Dedicated to the memory of Zora Arkus-Duntov

Zora Arkus-Duntov worked in the engineering department of Chevrolet Motor Division from 1953 to 1974. This 1954-55 Corvette history book is dedicated to him because of his influence in shaping and improving the Corvette, which began in this 1954-55 time frame.

Zora's contributions to the success of the Corvette cannot be overemphasized. His engineering talents and his enthusiasm for the Corvette combined to produce a list of accomplishments that compare favorably to the list of accomplishments produced by Harley Earl, the father of the Corvette.

Thanks, Mr. Duntov.

Thanks must go to my daughter, Lorraine, who helped nurse me through a difficult medical problem. All this time she was being a wife and mother.

Special thanks must also go to my daughter, Kim. Because I was in a wheelchair and unable to go downstairs to my office (and computer), Kim came every two weeks to be my typist. She put text and captions from notes into print, then brought them back for proofreading. This book would not have been possible without her skills.

Thanks to you all, I love each of you deeply.

Noland Adams

Corvette: American Le
1954-55 Prod

By Noland Adams

Published by : **Cars & Parts Magazine,** The Voice of the Collector Car Hobby Since 1957

Cars & Parts Magazine is a division of Amos Press Inc., 911 Vandemark Road, Sidney, Ohio

Also publishers of: Cars & Parts Collector Car Annual
Catalog of American Car ID Numbers 1950-59
Catalog of American Car ID Numbers 1960-69
Catalog of American Car ID Numbers 1970-79
Catalog of Camaro ID Numbers 1967-93
Catalog of Chevy Truck ID Numbers 1946-72
Catalog of Ford Truck ID Numbers 1946-72
Catalog of Chevelle, Malibu & El Camino ID Numbers 1964-87
Catalog of Pontiac GTO ID Numbers 1964-74
Catalog of Corvette ID Numbers 1953-93
Catalog of Mustang ID Numbers 1964$_{1/2}$-93
Catalog of Thunderbird ID Numbers 1955-93
Catalog of Firebird ID Numbers 1967-93
Catalog of Oldsmobile 4-4-2, W-Machine & Hurst/Olds ID Numbers 1964-91
Catalog of Chevy Engine V-8 Casting Numbers 1955-93
American Salvage Yard Treasures
Ultimate Collector Car Price Guide
Automobiles of America
Corvette: American Legend (The Beginning)

Printed and bound in the United States of America

Library of Congress Cataloging-In-Publication Date ISBN 1-880524-22-8

Volume 1 Review

In Volume 1, we followed the early planning and development of the General Motors sports car under the direction of Harley Earl, a GM vice president and the head of the GM Styling Studios. In complete secrecy, the prototype was built for the January 1953 GM Motorama. Called the Chevrolet Corvette by the time it was shown at the Motorama, the overwhelming public response was as GM management had hoped: many wanted to buy one.

At the Motorama, GM President Harlow Curtice announced that the Chevrolet Corvette would be in production in five and a half months! A building in Flint, Michigan, was prepared to assemble the first Corvettes on a short "pilot line."

In June of 1953 the Flint assembly line begin turning out fiberglass-bodied Corvettes. Production was slow because of the shortage of parts. The Corvette was introduced to the press in late September, followed by distribution to selected Chevrolet dealers.

The sales of new Corvettes were delayed to get as much publicity as possible. They were used in parades and public functions and displays of every type. Eventually, many were sold to high visibility celebrities and government officials.

The processes required to fabricate and assemble production fiberglass car bodies in 1953 was kept super secret by General Motors. This was a new system, and only employees were allowed in the assembly area. However, the entire assembly process was documented via photos, and we examined the entire assembly line in Volume 1.

While the Flint pilot line was producing a limited amount of 1953 Corvettes, plans were being made to operate a full 1954 production line in St. Louis, Missouri. The last 1953 Corvette was assembled in Flint on Thursday, Dec. 24, 1953. The first 1954 Corvette was assembled in St. Louis on Monday, Dec. 28, 1953. Fifteen 1954 Corvettes were assembled in St. Louis by year's end on Thursday, Dec. 31st.

Contents

1954
production begins

Chapter

1

The St. Louis assembly plant assembled Chevrolet passenger cars and trucks — and beginning with the 1954 model year — Corvettes too.

The St. Louis Chevrolet Assembly plant was notified in February 1953 to get ready to build metal-bodied Corvettes for the 1954 model year. The building selected was the old Mill Building, where wood bodies for Chevrolets were fabricated many years before.

March 28, 1953: The St. Louis Corvette Assembly Plant was still in its early planning stages when it was ordered to make a sudden change in direction. Based on the successes of fiberglass bodied test automobiles, and the Corvette production planned at the Flint pilot line, GM management had decided to build fiberglass-bodied Corvettes at St. Louis, instead of metal-bodied ones.

This decision was partly based on the projected lower tooling costs to produce the panels which would assemble the fiberglass body. At the time, this process of assembling a production fiberglass car body was unproven. But GM didn't hesitate: it was going to build 1,000 fiberglass-bodied Corvettes in St. Louis each month.

The late William L. Mosher, Jr., was the St. Louis plant manager. Shortly after the Flint line started assembling fiberglass Corvette bodies, Mr. Mosher sent 17 key assembly line personnel to the small Flint assembly line to observe the fiberglass body assembly process.

By any standard, the 1953 assembly line in Flint was small; about the size of two Kroger grocery stores. A shortage of parts kept 1953 production slow. Early in production, only one 1953 Corvette was completed every two days. Later, at the peak of production in late 1953, three were completed each day.

The Flint line was nothing more than a pilot line — a temporary, experience-gathering assembly line. It was never expected to provide more than the knowledge needed to order, modify and install the fabrication and assembly equipment for the much larger — and more productive — St. Louis Corvette assembly line.

The St. Louis plant managers used this opportunity well. They observed how the Flint assembly line functioned. There was no problem with the chassis line. There were only minor differences between the chassis assembly line in a Corvette plant compared to a Chevrolet passenger car line.

Assembling fiberglass Corvette bodies on such a large scale would require many new or modified fixtures. New conveyor systems, body assembling fixtures, tools for the body preparation areas, paint equipment, paint drying ovens and other specialized equipment were ordered. As they arrived, they were modified as necessary and installed in the old Mill building in the St. Louis assembly complex.

The 1953 plant in Flint completed its last unit, serial number 300, on Thursday, Dec. 24, 1953. Using the experience gained from the Flint operation, St. Louis was ready to build Corvettes. In fact, the Missouri plant produced the first 1954 Corvette on the next work day, Monday, Dec. 28, 1953. In total, the St. Louis plant assembled 15 1954 Corvettes before the end of 1953.

In the early months of 1954, the Chevrolet Corvette was a real novelty. Based on the prototype built for the Motorama, it was a fresh new design. Sales of new Corvettes (1953s and 1954s) were still restricted to persons in important positions, such as politicians, industry executives, movie stars — anyone with a high profile that "should be seen" in a new Corvette.

Of the 300 Corvettes built in Flint in 1953, only 183 were sold to these "special purchasers" by the end of 1953. Dealers who were fortunate to have a new Corvette available in 1953 or early 1954 used them to build traffic in the showroom. They were used in parades and every chance was taken to show off the new Corvette.

The 1953 sales figure of 183 was compared to the 1953 production figure of 315 units. In this context, the Corvette was considered a failure by the automotive press. However, it was too early to make a judgement on the public acceptance of the Corvette. One must keep in mind that sales of Corvettes were restricted to important persons.

1954 Corvette production in St. Louis began cautiously. The 15 units built in late 1953 took four days, about the production rate of the 1953 Flint assembly plant in the last days of December of 1953.

The St. Louis Corvette assembly plant began to pick up speed. Parts were arriving on a regular schedule; there were no more shortages. The St. Louis assembly line workers were

becoming more familiar with the special methods used to assemble a fiberglass car body. Efficiency within the plant was improving. The goal was 50 units per day, which would be about 1,000 per month. There was a long way to go, but it was a good start.

Just like the 1953 assembly line in Flint, the St. Louis Corvette assembly line was top secret. At the time the plant had all the secrecy of a stealth fighter assembly plant, the only difference being that one could see the new Corvettes that were being built.

Later, Chevrolet had photographers document the whole assembly line process. But for the time, it was a top secret facility.

William L. Mosher, Jr., manager of the St. Louis Chevrolet assembly plant, examines a model of the 1954 Corvette while actress Shirley Jones looks on during the 1954 Chicago Motorama.

A
brand
new
1954
Corvette
is about
to be
driven
away
from the
assembly
building.

1954 production in detail

Chapter

2

Production of a 1954 Corvette began with the installation of the underbody on a rotating fixture.

During 1953, the Old Mill Building at the St. Louis Chevrolet assembly plant was remodeled to assemble fiberglass-bodied Corvettes.

The late William Mosher, Jr., was the St. Louis plant manager. He had sent many key personnel to the Corvette pilot line operation at Flint to observe the special techniques required to assemble a fiberglass car body.

The St. Louis Corvette assembly plant was the first attempt to build fiberglass car bodies on a large scale. The process was so new that General Motors considered the body fabrication and assembly methods proprietary.

After the underbody was clamped to the fixture, it was rotated so 180 holes of various sizes could be drilled in the underbody.

As a result, information was rather guarded. That limited publicity, which the 1954 Corvette badly needed. During May, a photographer from GM Photographic was assigned the task of documenting the assembly line process.

In early June of 1954, Chevrolet was ready. It invited members of the automotive press to St. Louis. Forty reporters and writers were provided a new 1954 Corvette, which they drove across town to the Corvette assembly plant.

At the time, the assembly line, designed to produce a maximum of 50 units per day, was building 44 Corvettes per day. The members of the press saw the whole assembly line. At the end of the tour, Chevrolet provided them all with copies of the photos taken earlier by GM Photographic. None of the members of the press were allowed to photograph the assembly line — that's why photos were provided.

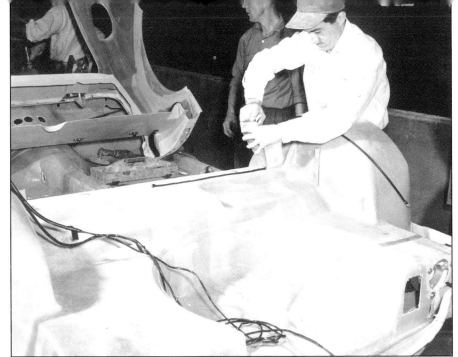

Assembly of the body began by squeezing an adhesive onto the underbody; the rear upper body sits in the background. Note the radio antenna lead behind the workers' arms.

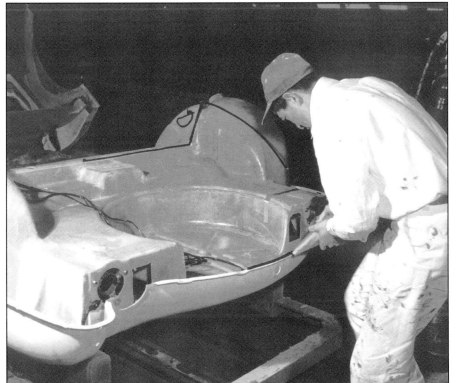

The adhesive called "bond" was squeezed onto the underbody's mounting flanges. Note the antenna lead, which would be glued in place permanently.

11

Once the rear upper body section was in place, the flanges were quickly clamped together.

Unfortunately, the publicity from the Corvette Plant's open house was too little, too late.

By late June, the assembly line was producing 50 units per day, as planned. But the large quantity of unsold Corvettes in dealers' showrooms and at the Corvette plant was just too much. Production was stopped for a couple of weeks at a time during the rest of 1954 production. Corvette assembly line workers were sent over to the nearby Chevrolet passenger car or pickup assembly plants.

While some assembly line workers finished mounting the rear upper body section, the exhaust outlets are prepared for installation.

Here, reinforcements are being installed, as the taillight pod awaits installation.

The assembly of the Corvette body continued (right) with the installation of panels and their hardware. Note that clamps were still on the front fender flanges.

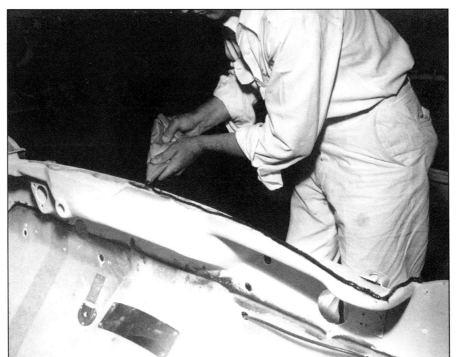

Bonding agent was applied on the top of the firewall prior to installing the dash. Note the hood latch mounted on the dash, the brackets and covers in place, and the radio antenna lead pushed through a couple of holes.

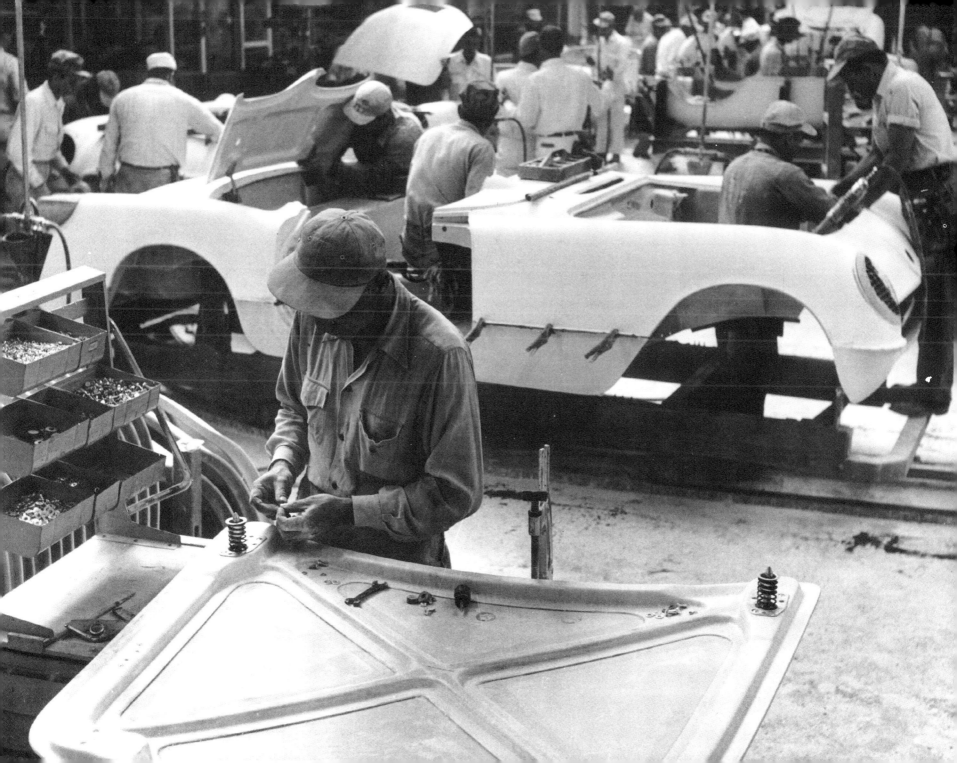

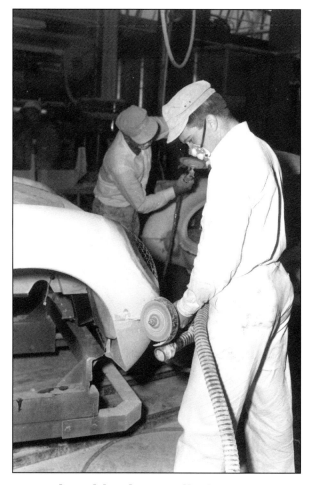

Completed bodies, called "bodies in white," were prepared by grinding away all oversized areas.

Hand sanding Corvette bodies: Note the "Corvette" shirts. An oft-voiced question is why the workers were not wearing dust masks. This was a Mahon water-back booth, where air flows from above, over the work surfaces and workers, then into a water bath below, through the water and back through the booth. Thus the air was water-filtered and dust free.

At right: Primer was sprayed-on, the bodies were hand sanded. The workers were not wearing masks because the air powered "jitterbug" sanders also had a constant water supply. Note the colored bodies on the opposite line.

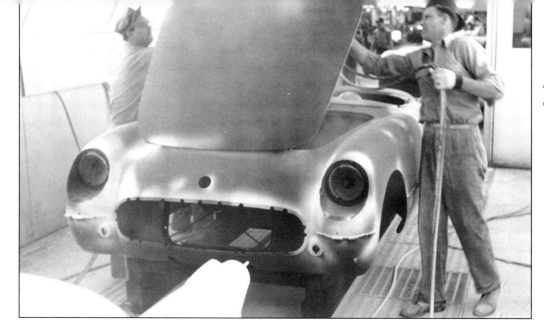

Applying the first color coat.

Applying the first color coat, followed by a trip through the sanding line, then into the final color coat application.

18

**Final color coat
application.**

**Final color coat application. Note the lower grilles,
part of the Mahon water-back booth.**

After the bodies were painted, hardware was installed: Here Jim Snelson selects a gas tank.

At right. Wiring harnesses and other goodies are shown being installed (right). Note the uneven paint line on the left edge of the hood.

The windshield and other hardware were then installed.

Installation of the folding top on the final trim line: that's Charles E. Cummins wearing a cap.

The end of the final trim line. Note the goodies on the right, including a grille assembly.

A brand new Corvette engine and Powerglide transmission await installation in a chassis.

In an industry first, Corvette wheels were balanced on the assembly line using a Hunter balancing machine.

A new Corvette chassis — ready to run — awaits the body drop.

The Hunter balancer at work on the front wheel.

An overview of the balancer's framework.

The balancing technique.

1954 Corvette body drop. Note the dirty whitewall and no wheel covers.

Body drop of a blue 1954 Corvette. Note the dirty whitewalls, and the wheel covers in place.

The final inspection line at the St. Louis assembly plant.

Another new Corvette comes off the end of the assembly line.

Inspecting a new 1954 Corvette are (from left) R.G. Ford, manager of Chevrolet assembly plants; William L. Mosher, Jr., manager of the St. Louis assembly plants; and E.H. Kelley, general manufacturing manager of the Chevrolet Motor Division. This photo was posed in May of 1954.

New 1954 Corvettes await shipment to dealers in the St. Louis storage lot. The tops appear to be wrinkled, but those are actually paper shipping covers. Note the new Chevrolet passenger cars coming from the assembly building in the background.

Loading up another truck load of new Corvettes.

Duntov's exhaust studies

Chapter

3

The Corvette was originally designed as a dream car. When the 1953 Corvette went into production, it retained all the strengths and weaknesses of the original dream car.

The owners of 1953 and early 1954 Corvettes complained about exhaust debris staining the rear of their otherwise gleaming white Corvette bodies. Also, there were complaints about exhaust fumes in the passenger compartment under certain conditions. The problem was with the location of the exhaust outlets. They were originally designed to look good on the prototype dream car, but they caused problems on cars that were driven on a regular basis.

Early in 1954, these problems were referred to an assistant staff engineer named Zora Arkus-Duntov.

These days it would be easy to trace air flow — we'd just put the car in a wind tunnel. Duntov didn't have such a device available, so he improvised.

First, he applied strips of cloth all over the body. Then he drove the Corvette at a moderate speed, while a photographer in another car took 16mm movies of the cloth strips under different conditions.

When Duntov viewed the films, he found a "dead" air flow area all around the rear of the body. Exhaust gasses and common road debris were trapped in this area. Eventually some of the exhaust particles and debris stuck to the body. This was causing the annoying staining of the paint in that area.

Duntov tried several combinations to determine how exhaust fumes got into the passenger compartment. He raised and lowered the folding top, and installed and removed the side curtains.

The movies pointed to the culprit. With the folding top raised, the side curtains installed, and the vent window about one-third open, a low-pressure area developed. Exhaust gasses that had collected at the rear of the body were drawn forward through the partially opened vent window.

The quick fix was to modify the tail pipe outlet, officially called an extension. The original design was a straight piece of chrome plated pipe which extended past the body about two inches. Duntov's solution was a new, longer extension, almost six inches long. Plus, the rear opening of the extension was capped. Instead of a straight outlet there was an internal baffle which directed exhaust gasses through a slot in the lower half of the extension.

Short exhaust.

The new, longer exhaust outlet did not cure all the problems. It did cause exhaust gasses to be directed down, into the air flow. The rear of the body was stained less, plus exhaust gasses were eliminated from the passenger compartment. Some road debris and dust could still remain in the dead air flow area behind the car, but this was considered to be a minimal problem.

The longer exhaust extension became a running change (not a model year change) during mid-1954 Corvette production. The longer extensions were installed during the remainder of the 1954 model year run, and all during 1955 production.

The 1956 Corvette exhaust outlet design was changed because of Duntov's 1954 tests. The outlets were moved to the center of the rear bumper on each side. The exhaust gasses were carried away in the moving air stream.

The exhaust outlet's location stayed in this area from 1956 through 1960 production. Then the location moved again, and it has moved many times since. Perhaps Chevrolet engineers are still looking for the perfect location.

The solution: Long exhaust.

More
horsepower

Corvette engineers have always had a battle over horsepower ratings. The prototype had been rated at 160 hp. When production of 1953 Corvettes was announced, test vehicles were equipped with the 160-hp version of the Corvette six-cylinder. But the 160-hp version was too touchy. Something in those early engines was changed (maybe the compression was lowered) so the six-cylinder engines were rated at an honest 150 hp.

The engine group looked for a way to get more horsepower for the Corvette. They finally found room for improvement in the camshaft. By opening the valves sooner and closing them later, engine horsepower increased 5 hp.

As we all know, 5 hp is not a big increase, but this was a "solid" increase. That is, you could feel the power — especially the acceleration between the 150 and 155 versions. The 155-hp version definitely had sharper performance.

From the 1954 National Service Data:

"Camshaft: note 1953 and early 1954 camshafts are different than later 1954 camshafts. Later type camshafts are identified by three large raised dots located between #5 and #6 inlet cams." The raised dots are also located on the front end of the camshaft.

Five horsepower is no big deal if the engine is already pumping out 300+ hp. But add a solid 5 hp to a 150-hp engine, and it does help.

The camshaft shown here is the original one from E54S002042 the 2,042nd 1954 Corvette built with engine number 04549334F54YG. As far as we know this is the first 1954 Corvette to achieve the high horsepower rating of 155!

Prototype V-8 engine installation in 1954

Chapter

5

For many years, Chevrolet engines were four or six in-line cylinders, water cooled, with overhead valves. There had been variations, including an air-cooled engine and even a V-8, but we're ignoring them here.

Several GM Divisions (like the 1949 Oldsmobile Rocket) had been developing overhead valve V-8 engines. In the early fifties, the Chevrolet V-8 was materializing. There were many little technical problems, but they were being solved. The new V-8 would be introduced in passenger cars at the beginning of the 1955 model year.

There had not been any statements made about the 1955 Corvette power plant. Members of the automotive press were beginning to wonder — in print — if Corvette would get a V-8 engine.

But the Corvette engineers were just cautious. They had pulled a 1954 Corvette off the St. Louis assembly line and trucked it to the GM Tech Center. The six-cylinder engine was pulled and replaced by a prototype V-8.

This was not an operational engine. It was installed to check for clearances between the engine and its components, and the body frame. There were many dummy parts, such as the air cleaner, which was the correct size but was made of wood.

One interference problem was evident. The fuel pump touched the frame. The solution was to bend the frame to pro-

1955 PROTOTYPE —

NOTE 6 CYL. CHOKE CABLES

vide a notch in the frame. The V-8 fuel pump cleared the frame, and the V-8 now fit the Corvette chassis.

Using this test installation, Chevrolet decided the V-8 would fit in the Corvette. Late in 1954, without a major announcement, the V-8 was going to be available in all 1955 Chevrolets, including the Corvette. It was a good decision, for the V-8 engine at 195 hp was 28 pounds lighter than the six-cylinder Chevrolet engine at 155 hp.

Manufacturing
1954 panels at MFG

Cleaning perforated screen for making rear upper part of body.

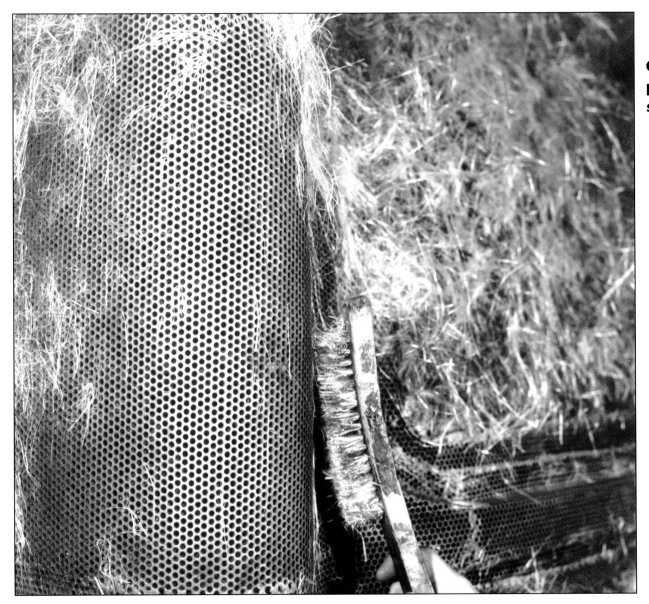

Close-up of perforated screen.

At right. Blowing resin and chopped glass on screen: Vacuum holds material in place as platform turns around.

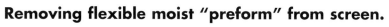
Removing flexible moist "preform" from screen.

At top left: Preform is placed in lower mold, stretched in place, resin is added, then dies are closed and heated. Here the dies have just opened.

At bottom left: Removing completed part from dies.

Sanding, trimming and inspecting parts prior to shipment. A blank panel covers the gas filler area, showing the correct body contours.

Chopper gun mixes chopped fiberglass and resin and blows it on the screen: Vacuum holds the material in place. This station is making a set of taillight pods.

Taillight pods being sanded and inspected prior to shipment to the St. Louis assembly plant.

Stacks of parts are being sanded, trimmed and inspected prior to shipment. The station in the foreground is finishing the inner hood support braces.

Motorama, Jan. 20, 1954 – New York

Chapter

7

XP-34
4 DR "FOUR SEATER" RUNABOUT

We profiled Carl Renner in Volume One. During Carl's career with Harley Earl's design studios he drew many cars over a span of many years. A number of them donated details — some minor, some major — to many GM designs. We were fortunate to obtain several Renner drawings from the early fifties. The LaSalle II-XP 34 was one concept for a roadster. The flying rear fender was to show up on the Buick Wildcat II. The side cove was used on several dream cars, and the 1956 Corvette. The fastback reminds us of the Chevrolet Corvair dream car.

There must have been hundreds of drawings produced by Harley Earl's GM styling studios in the early fifties. Many talented artists worked to create new designs. A total vehicle's design is the result of a subtle curved line, or perhaps bold changes to a fender line. Minor details were selected from many drawings, then the original drawings were routinely destroyed.

Few of these original drawings from the early fifties exist today. Fortunately for us, several early renderings (shaded drawings) by Carl Renner survived. Both had special features that were used on future GM dream cars and/or production cars.

Pontiac had a Corvette-sized dream car at the 1954 GM Motorama called the Bonneville Special. It was named after the Bonneville salt flats in Utah, the site of many land speed record attempts. Its body was fiberglass, powered by a Pontiac straight 8 with four sidedraft carburetors. The Bonneville special shared its rounded front fenders and recessed headlights with the Corvette. This headlight treatment can be traced back through Corvette to Henry Lauve's 1943 drawing as seen in Volume One.

In this version of XP 34, Renner's design was used, as intended, on the LaSalle II roadster. Renner used many different front name-plates, with "Cougar" shown here. Sometimes the car was a "R-E-N-N-E-R" named after the artist.

This version of the XP 34 is similar to the LaSalle II roadster except for the front end. This shows a special name: the GM initials with a lightning bolt through the center.

The XP-34 proposal is again like the LaSalle II roadster with a different front end and an unknown front emblem.

The Bonneville's body style was a two seat coupe with center-hinged windows that lifted straight up to get into the car. This was first seen on Carl Renner's "Chevrolet Corvette 'Skylite'."

Buick's Corvette-sized dream car for 1954 was called Wildcat II. When the original Wildcat was shown at the 1953 Motorama, it had no number designation. But with the 1954 appearance of Wildcat II, the original 1953 show car now became Wildcat I.

The 1954 Wildcat II was a fiberglass bodied two-seat convertible with several unusual features. The taillights were described by the automotive press as derivatives of the Corvette taillight. Although they were mounted in the same approximate location, they were not mounted on a pod exactly like the Corvette. Therefore, it is not easily recognizable as a Corvette descendant.

Wildcat II is best known for its recessed front and rear side coves behind the tires. The side cove heritage can be traced back to Carl Renner's 1956 Corvette proposal

This XP-34 rendering has no visible numbers. This version is very close to the LaSalle II dream car, minus the brushed side cove inserts.

#3 CHEVROLET CORVETTE "SKYLITE"

ReNNer

This rendering was redrawn from the faded original by this writer, so some lines do not intersect properly. This is the Chevrolet Corvette "Skylite" which featured many innovations to be used on later models. The hinged upper entry panels (windows?) were seen later on the 1954 Pontiac Bonneville dream car. The reverse side coves were used on the 1955 Chevrolet Biscayne dream car, and the Chevrolet Corvair. The ducktail rear end was used on the 1960 production Chevrolet Corvair and the 1961 Corvette. The windsplit (front to rear peak on the center of the trunk lid) was used on the 1961 Corvette.

This rendering shows front and rear side coves, as used on the 1954 Buick Wildcat II dream car. The grille looks like the 1956 Buick Centurion dream car grille, and the 1961 Corvette grille.

drawn in 1953. This side cove treatment was used on several dream cars in 1955, and on the production Corvette in 1956.

Another introduction on the Wildcat II was trunk mounted chrome trim. This later appeared on production Corvettes in 1958 as the two long "trunk spears."

Oldsmobile produced the F-88, a two-seat fiberglass-bodied convertible. The open-mouthed grille appeared on later full sized Olds — in the mid-fifties. The F-88's taillights were very much like the Corvette's, being mounted high on long pods.

The question could now be asked "how did dream cars from four different GM divisions come to share certain styling variations?" This is an especially puzzling question when one considers the tight security. All of the styling studios were locked, and only studio heads and styling's upper management were allowed in another division's studios. This secrecy was emphasized when we interviewed designers Henry Lauve and Carl Renner for this series of books. Although they knew each other, neither was aware of what was done by the other one. They simply did not discuss their work with anyone. So ... if the security was so effective, how did the designs from one studio get shared by other GM studios?

There had to be one connecting link. There was. It was Harley Earl, a vice president of GM and the head of the GM styling studios.

Clearly, Mister Earl was lord and master of the GM styling studios in the early fifties. Mister Earl started the idea of the GM sports car, which became the Corvette. Again using his talented staff, including Lauve and Renner, he began designing a new herd of dream cars for the 1954 Motorama.

Mister Earl was a tall, authoritative figure. His work designing automobiles had earned him a reputation for producing quality designs. This respect for his work earned him the top spot in the GM studios, where Mister Earl was a tough boss. He demanded a lot from his studio staff, yet anyone who produced quality work got along with Mister Earl just fine.

There were seven design studios: Chevrolet, Pontiac, Buick, Oldsmobile, Cadillac, Advanced Design and Trucks. Each of the GM division studios functioned independently. Many nights, long after the designers and stylists and clay modelers and studio heads had gone home for the evening, Mister Earl visited each design studio. He was the final authority on each design. To assure that his wishes were carried out, Mister Earl wrote notes of approval or disapproval or suggestions on the drawings.

Since his notes carried the highest possible regard, Mister Earl was often referred to as "God." But not when Mister Earl could hear the comment. The styling studio employees joked that if God himself were to visit GM, he would have to get Mister Earl's permission.

So each design studio — Chevrolet, Pontiac, Buick and Oldsmobile — followed Mister Earl's directions. Since Mister Earl was the Father of the Corvette, he used a section here and there from the original Corvette design. Sharing a front fender curve on one car, and a taillight design on another, these dream cars had their own identity, but revealed their Corvette heritage.

Besides the Corvette-sized Buick Wildcat II, Oldsmobile F-88, and Pontiac Bonneville Special, there were three Chevrolet dream cars, all directly related to the Corvette. The best known is the Corvette Nomad. Since it was introduced at the GM Motorama at the Waldorf Astoria Hotel in New York City, it has also become known as the Waldorf Nomad.

Bodywise, it was a smaller, lower car, with a fiberglass

body. The entire front end was Corvette, with the distinctive Corvette taillights on extended mounting pods in the rear. It was powered by a Corvette six-cylinder engine. Like many GM dream cars, the car ran rather poorly. All the development time had been used on the body fit and finish. The engine ran well enough to move the car around shows, but it was not a truly roadworthy car. Stories tell of a test lap around the Milford (Michigan) test track, the GM Proving Ground. The Corvette Nomad got up enough speed to make one lap, which was good enough for a dream car that was to be driven occasionally for a short distance.

The 1954 Motorama showcased among other things the Firebird (front). Behind it is the Pontiac Bonneville Special. The seating area for the orchestra can be seen in the upper right.

On turntables (left to right) are the Pontiac Bonneville, GM Firebird, and Buick Wildcat II. The top curtain is closed. The name Firebird wasn't used by Pontiac until the late sixties, specifically the 1967 model year.

When the Corvette Nomad appeared at the GM Motorama in January of 1954, it proved to be a real crowd pleaser. The late Claire "Mac" MacKichian was the head of the Chevrolet studio at the time. As the design management folks prepared to leave New York City and return to Detroit, Mac called the Chevrolet studios. Carl Renner was Mac's assistant, and Mac told Carl that the Nomad roofline was going into production on a regular Chevrolet station wagon body. It was fitting that Carl Renner got that call. The original concept was to build a dream car station wagon with a telescoping roof ... almost like a station wagon convertible.

Carl Renner's roof design was selected, and he has been celebrated for that roof design. However, the roof panels were fixed, not telescoping, because of the expense, and the potential for a leakage problem. However, Renner's horizontal creases and slanted door posts remained and became a Nomad trademark.

After Mac's phone call, Carl Renner removed the full sized Corvette Nomad drawing from its display board. He cut the station wagon roof off the drawing and trimmed and taped it to a full-sized drawing of a 1955 regular Chevrolet station wagon. By the time the design management folks arrived back in town, Renner had completed the design work.

The Pontiac Bonneville Special models the center hinged entry windows which originated on Carl Renner's Corvette "Skylite."

The Pontiac Bonneville Special dream car used rounded front fenders and recessed headlights just like the Corvette.

This is the stylish two-seater 1953 Buick Wildcat dream car. When the Wildcat II debuted in 1954, this 1953 version was thereafter known as Wildcat I.

The markedly different Wildcat II of 1954.

The other Corvette-based dream car shown at the 1954 Motorama was the Corvair, a two-seat fastback coupe. It resembled a 1966 Mustang upper body grafted onto a 1954 Corvette, with minor exterior trim changes. This was the first use of the name Corvair on a Chevrolet design. The next use of the name was the production car, the 1960 to 1969 rear engined Chevrolet Corvair.

The 1954 dream car Corvair first appeared in a cherry red paint job. By the time the car arrived at the Los Angeles Motorama, two months later, it had been repainted a light green.

The Buick Wildcat II.

Buick Wildcat II

The Oldsmobile F-88 dream car.

This completes the list of 1954 Motorama special dream cars shown in New York City in January. When the Motorama opened in Miami in February, the last "dream car" joined the Motorama show on the road. This was a 1953 Corvette, modified to accept a removable hardtop. The installation of a special windshield frame was required to accommodate the hardtop mounting and sealing. The doors were modified with the addition of external door buttons and roll-up windows. With the hardtop removed, only the external door buttons suggested that this might be a special car.

While the 1953 Corvette with the removable hardtop was a special prototype, it was never called a dream

The Oldsmobile F-88's massive front grille.

car. The hardtop — with different mounting hardware — was installed as a factory option at the start of 1956 Corvette production.

How Many and Where Are They Now?

This writer has always been curious about how many of these dream cars were built, and how many still exist. First, we must examine the dream car construction process. All designs start with a series of drawings and renderings. Renderings are drawings shaded to show depth and details.

After a promising design is selected, a drawing is made, and a small (maybe 1/4) scale model is crafted in clay. If this design is approved, a full-sized drawing is made, followed by a full-sized clay model. By this time there have been many hours of work invested.

The full-sized clay is trimmed and smoothed to the final size and shape. When the design is finalized, a mold is made directly off the full-sized clay by laying sheets of cloth and plaster over it. The clay is removed, and recycled to be used on the next clay model.

The plaster mold has layers of fiberglass layed in and smoothed, then satu-

Interior layout of the F-88 cockpit.

rated with resin. This results in a one-piece fiberglass body. The hood, trunk, doors and instrument mounting holes must be cut into the body.

Due to the concave design of some one-piece bodies, the plaster mold must be cut or broken to remove the completed body. It was common practice to

The F-88 was a fully functional car, and was driven to many races as an example of GM styling's work. Note how the taillight sits on an extended pod, similar to the Corvette's design.

repair the plaster mold and produce two, sometimes three, prototype bodies from the same mold.

For example, three copies of the Pontiac Bonneville Special were built. Two exist in private hands.

We don't know much about the Wildcat II, but we heard one existed in private hands.

The Oldsmobile F-88 was one of the most attractive dream cars. Three were built, and all exist in private hands. This writer had a chance to see, smell and touch (gently) one of the F-88s.

Apparently only one Corvette Nomad and one Corvair were built. As far as we know, the originals were destroyed.

Two Corvettes were modified to become removable hard-top prototypes: one to tour the U.S., which was painted light yellow. The second, painted green, toured Canada. Apparently the yellow U.S. car was destroyed. The green Canadian Motorama hardtop car is in private hands in Canada.

The Corvette Nomad is shown on display in the styling studios. There is a Corvette hood emblem in the center of each wheelcover. An article in the April 1954 issue of *Car Life* captioned this photo "unusually unusual ... or perhaps just wierd" ... Chevrolet's experimental Corvette station wagon.

Interior of the Corvette Nomad.

Despite reports
that the rear
window was
non-functional, it
did work as
shown here.

The Corvette Nomad's
tailgate functioned, as
did the seats, which
folded down like a
regular station wagon.

The Chevrolet Corvair fastback was painted cherry red for the first 1954 Motorama shows.

The rear of the Biscayne dream car shows features that will surface on future Chevrolets. The overall look was used on the 1960 Corvair. The license plate frame and rear bumpers were used on the 1961 to 1967 Corvettes.

Unloading the Biscayne dream car for the GM Motorama at the Waldorf-Astoria Hotel in New York City. Note the covers over the tires.

The 1955 Biscayne dream car shows features of future Chevrolets. The side cove can be traced back to Renner's drawings for the LaSalle II dream cars. It's reversed here, with the name "Chevrolet" in the side cove, which would be used on fuel-injected Corvettes.

Front end of the Biscayne dream car. The grille teeth can be traced back to Renner's drawing. The Chevrolet studio's staff at the time was "Mac" MacKichian, studio chief; Bob Semanski, assistant chief, and designers Carl Renner and Bob Cadaret.

GM Motorama
in Miami

Chapter

8

The 1954 Corvette with the prototype removable hardtop.

The General Motors Motorama was a show of enormous proportions. The Motoramas were based on car shows that began shortly after the turn of the century. Back then, car shows were planned to get all the current production cars in one area so the public could see (and buy) the latest in automobiles. Smaller manufacturers might have a single example on display.

The biggest auto shows were held in New York City or Detroit, but every major city had its own auto show. Auto shows and automobile production were interrupted by World War II, when they were replaced by military vehicle production. After the war, the American public was driving used cars. It took a couple of years to return to building regular automobiles.

Right after the war, in the late forties and early fifties, it was easy to sell new cars. The demand was so great that there were waiting lists at each dealer. It was impossible to simply walk into a new car dealership and buy a car — you were placed on the waiting list.

By 1951 and 1952, though, supply had caught up with demand. Auto shows were coming back to every major city, where all models from all manufacturers were on display. Upper management at General Motors had always supported auto shows. GM decided to promote its cars by having its own auto show.

The show would be named the General Motors Motorama, and the first one would be in 1953. All the equipment — raised platforms, turntables, fences, etc. were designed to be portable. After the show opened in January in New York City, it traveled to several other cities. The cities varied, but each year's circuit always started in New York City and included Miami, Los Angeles and San Francisco.

But this was more than a display of currently available GM production cars. GM's styling studios had built a couple of special cars to test the public's reaction. Although a couple of years old, these "dream cars" were relatively unknown outside GM circles.

The styling studios designed and built several dream cars for the 1953 Motorama. One was the Corvette prototype.

But the Motorama organizers weren't done yet. There was an orchestra — a full-sized one — and a chorus — a big one, and dancers and singers, just like a Broadway production. Then there were displays from all the GM divisions. These displays might be phone booth sized functional systems — like suspension, or maybe a power steering system with a steering wheel with which to play.

The whole Motorama operation took several days to set up or tear down. It took a fleet of 110 to 125 Chevy or GMC trucks to move it between cities.

Of course the public liked the Motorama. There were displays of the dream cars. There were displays of GM production cars. There were dream car and production car brochures. There were mechanical displays from many GM divisions. There was an orchestra, a chorus, and singers and dancers. A really big show, and it was all FREE.

The GM design staff had modified a 1953 Corvette to accept a removable hardtop which was shown at the Miami Motorama for the first time. This required a new windshield frame to mount the hardtop. Without side curtains, which had a vent window (to reach the doorknob), there was a special outside door pushbutton. This allowed roll-up windows, but the interior door pockets were eliminated. A glove box was located in the kick panel. It was small, so the name "glove box" is fitting.

One display was intended to illustrate the flexible qualities of fiberglass. A 1954 Corvette rear fender was mounted inside a showcase behind glass. A hammer was menacingly aimed at the rear panel. Linkage connected the hammer to a handle mounted on the side of the display case.

Of course the hammer was aimed at a flat, flexible area, so it was not likely one could damage the rear panel. At the time the photo on page 76 was taken, the counter had registered 71,561 cycles (hits on the panel).

A small "glove box" was built into the kick panels.

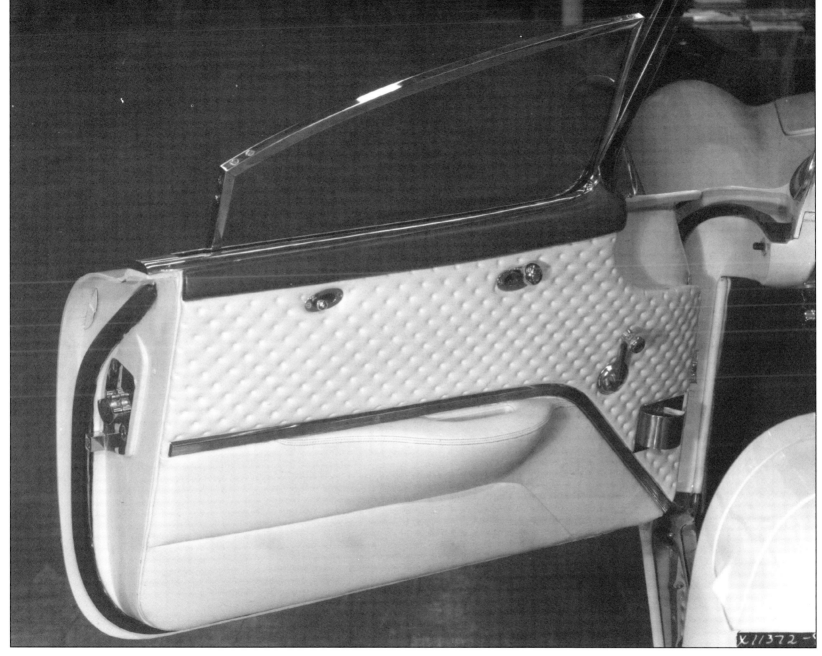

The doors were modified to contain a window crank mechanism, which required a new door panel.

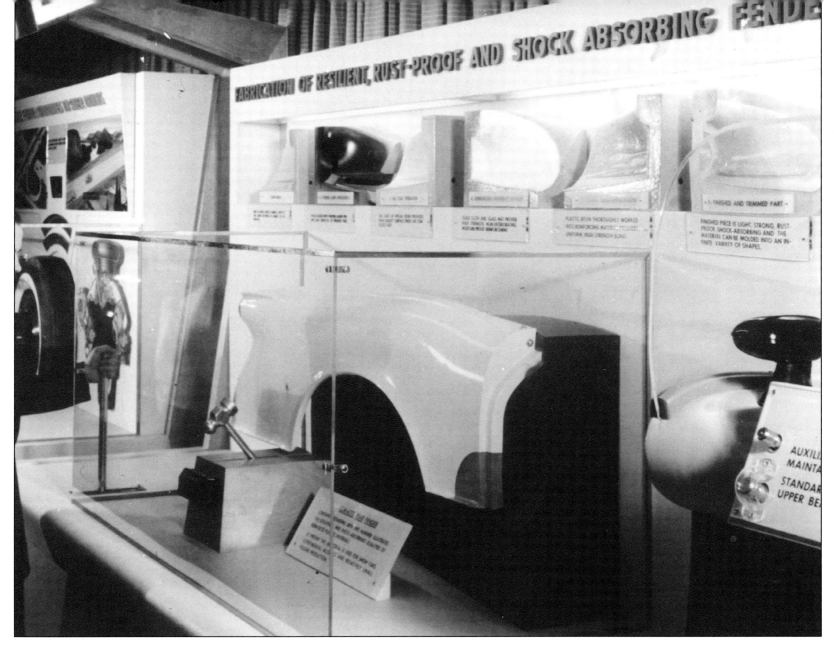

Motorama display demonstrated the flexible qualities of fiberglass.

Rear view details features of the Motorama show car.

With the top removed, the car looked like a production '54, except for the pushbutton doors and hood emblems in the center of the wheel covers.

GM Motorama
in Los Angeles

Chapter

9

It took a large fleet of Chevrolet and GMC trucks to move the GM Motorama cars and equipment. To avoid traffic problems, the trucks traveled in small convoys of 10 or 12 trucks at a time. The drivers kept in touch via a radio/telephone setup, fairly rare in 1955.

The 1954 GM Motorama was playing to large crowds. And why not. There were dream cars, production cars, an orchestra, a chorus, singers and dancers, and technical exhibits.

One of the most successful 1954 dream cars was the Corvette Nomad. The roof style had already been ordered into production on a standard Chevrolet station wagon body.

When the Corvette Nomad dream car reached Los Angeles, it had suffered a bit of body damage. There was one person in Los Angeles who was experienced with fiberglass body repair. We tracked him down, and he remembered repairing the Corvette Nomad. As I recall, it had been tapped in a rear corner.

The L.A. body man repaired and painted the Corvette Nomad. He took quite a few pictures, but he gave them away one at a time, and they were all gone. When I asked him the condition of the Corvette Nomad, he replied "rough."

The Corvair was painted cherry red for its introduction at the New York City Motorama. It was repainted light green for the Los Angeles Motorama.

While in Los Angeles, three of the Motorama cars were driven to a circular section of a parking lot for a photo session. A production Corvette with its top down, the Corvette Nomad, the Corvair fastback, and the Corvette with a removable hardtop were all there. All smiled for the camera.

Rows of Chevrolet and GMC Motorama trucks at rest during the Los Angeles Motorama. It took 100 to 125 semis to move the Motorama from city to city.

Unloading 1954 Motorama dream cars in Los Angeles. Front to rear: Cadillac El Camino, Pontiac Strato Star and Chevrolet Corvette Nomad.

The Chevrolet Corvette Corvair fastback coupe, shown before in cherry red, has been repainted a light green. Note the hood emblems in the center of the wheel covers.

The Motorama is ready for the public. Examples of then current GM production cars sit on the floor. On the turntables: left front, a production Buick Skylark convertible; slightly to the right and in the rear, a production 1954 Corvette; center front, Buick Wildcat II; five production convertibles (one from each GM division) on the large turntable; right front, Chevrolet Corvette Nomad; next turntable, Pontiac Bonneville; right center, Oldsmobile Cutlass, and, directly the behind, the Oldsmobile F-88.

The Corvette-based dream cars plus one. Front to rear: Corvair fastback, Corvette Nomad, the removable hardtop car, and in the left rear, a production Corvette.

Le Mans, France 1954

Based on an interview by Jerry McDermott

Chapter
10

Zora Arkus-Duntov was born to Russian parents in Brussels, Belgium on December 25, 1909. That wasn't his original name. His mother divorced and remarried while he was young; the name Zora Arkus-Duntov combined his father's and stepfather's names.

Zora Arkus-Duntov has become commonly known as "Mr. Duntov" or "Duntov." From here on, we will use "Duntov."

Duntov showed an interest in mechanical devices. He was befriended by a Russian general, who supplied him several surplus aircraft and other engines. Duntov had an excellent knowledge of internal-combustion engines while still in his teens.

Duntov's mechanical knowledge and his interest in racing led him to specialized work at many companies. His talented hand touched such diverse companies as Allard, Jaguar, Mercedes-Benz, Pegaso, Porsche, Volkswagen and, of course, General Motors.

Duntov takes the checkered flag at the 1954 LeMans, winning the 1100cc class. Behind him is the 1500cc Porsche, which won its class also.

The thirties found Duntov in Berlin where he undertook formal education in engineering. During his undergraduate days, he assisted fellow student Hans Joachim Bernard, who would become a cham-pionship race car driver. During this time, he published a technical paper suggesting a method to minimize the stress placed on a supercharged engine by the compressor. The paper drew the attention of one individual who assisted Duntov in starting a company to produce and sell the product under the VD nameplate.

Duntov's relationship with Porsche started with a meeting with Dr. Ferdinand Porsche in 1937 when they discussed the Auto Union race cars. Some theoretical design studies resulted from this meeting, but nothing significant came from this encounter.

In 1939, Duntov moved to France where he became involved in racing. When that activity was disrupted by the Nazi invasion, he joined the French Air Force, only to be discharged a short time later when France surrendered. Crossing Spain, Duntov made his way to Portugal where he was able to obtain passage to New York, arriving there by ship on December 4, 1940.

Having skills and needing funds, Duntov was ready to go to work but had difficulty because of his limited use of English. One of his friends from Germany, Julian Hoffman, suggested that he become a manufacturer. After the Japanese attack on Pearl Harbor, he started manufacturing bullets in the "Hells Kitchen" section of New York City. A short time later he switched to aircraft parts as a subcontractor for Remington Rand who, with Hamilton Standard, made 30 percent of the propellers for the war effort. Starting with only five people, his work force had grown to 300 by the end of the war.

After the war, there was little demand for these products so Duntov reduced his staff and turned to making products to increase performance in automotive engines. The budding interest in hot rods focused attention on the Ardun overhead valve conversion kit for flathead Ford engines, which he manufactured with his brother.

The Ardun heads used the name derived from Arkus-Duntov. They made the Ford flathead engine look like a Chrysler hemi. The resultant Ardun conversion engine was a strong, competitive powerplant.

With Duntov's reputation for being able to improve engine performance, he was approached by Sidney Allard from England. Allard was building a series of sports cars using large American V-8 engines. Duntov's sojourn at Allard was not limited to the laboratory as he drove full-bodied Allards at the LeMans 24-hour race in 1952 and 1953.

During his time at Allard, Duntov had published an article in an English technical journal regarding the use of mini-tests to extrapolate car data. It suggested a significant change from the accepted practice at that time. It was due to this paper that he was hired by General Motors, but in the meantime, he had returned to the United States to work for Fairchild Aviation.

His career with General Motors started on May 1, 1953 as an assistant staff engineer. Although he was assigned routine assignments (like designing a school bus driveline), he found time to be around the Corvette as it developed. Whenever an assistant engineer was needed to do some testing on the Corvette, Duntov got the job.

This writer knew the Duntovs well enough to visit them at their home several times. The last time I was in their home was four months before Zora died. I had stopped by on short notice, and hadn't planned on staying for dinner.

While Elfi cooked dinner, Zora and I talked. I had asked all the Corvette questions I could think of many years ago. So we talked about his new airplane, a BD5. This is a tiny home-built plane with a pusher engine (the jet version is called the BD5J).

Zora was intent on setting a new speed record for small propeller driven aircraft. One of the shops at GM was modifying a Suzuki 3-cylinder engine (as used in the Geo Metro). Zora had carefully calculated everything. He was an experienced pilot with a new speed record in the Guinness Book of World Records as his goal. The engine modification work was not completed on time, so the attempt was never made.

While we talked about the work on his BD5, the phone rang. It was a writer returning Zora's call. This writer had written something about Corvettes. Although I couldn't hear the conversation, it was clear Zora was upset, and he lost no time criticizing the writer's comments about the Corvette. More than 20 years after retirement, Zora Arkus-Duntov still protected the Corvette like it was his personal car.

Over the years, I had seen many engineering reports, articles and internal memos written by Duntov. All were clear and concise and showed that he had a good technical understanding of the English language. Add in his racing experiences — both as mechanic and driver — and the result was an engineer who could diagnose most any problem, then write a detailed technical report about the solution.

Back to the McDermott interview: Duntov soon rose to engineering manager of High Performance Cars and later became chief engineer for Corvette. Along the way, he set a speed record for American cars at Daytona Beach.

Experienced race car drivers with an engineering background — like Duntov — were in great demand. On February 23, 1954, Duntov received a letter from Porsche which stated, "We are acknowledging receipt of your letter of February 16 to Mr. von Hanstein and learned with pleasure that you would be interested in driving one of our cars in the LeMans race."

On April 5, 1954, Duntov received another letter from Porsche, "We are interested in having you on our official Porsche Team." A 1089cc Spyder would be available for Duntov. "The car will be fully equal to the other Porsches and fitted with the new overhead cam engine which develops about 90 hp, thus giving excellent performance and we think, the utmost of reliability." The letter was signed by Huschke von Hanstein, the team manager, and Dr. Ferry Porsche.

A few weeks later, Porsche again wrote to Duntov expressing pleasure that he would be part of the team and advising him to arrive in LeMans, "not later than the 9th of June to give you the possibility to try out the car in the meantime."

Duntov was scheduled to drive with Hans Herrmann, another Porsche team driver. However, with international goodwill at stake, he was paired with Olivier, a Frenchman, in number 47, the only 550 Spyder with the 1089cc engine. Olivier was a friend of Auguste Veuillet who influenced Porsche's LeMans participation. Veuillet would become Duntov's co-driver for the LeMans race the following year.

Trivia buffs should note the small capacity of the engine in Duntov's car as the other Porsches were entered with the 1500cc version of the four-cam engine. The 1089cc engine produced 72 bhp at approximately 7000 rpm, which translates to more than one horsepower per cubic inch.

Chevrolet's engineering management was headed up by chief engineer Ed Cole. Duntov's direct supervisor was

In the pits, Duntov is surrounded by a happy crew, including his wife, Elfi.

Maurice Olley. Cole and Olley agreed to give Duntov time off from his duties as an assistant staff engineer to go to the LeMans race.

In return, Duntov observed the engineering progress of Porsche — and other manufacturers — and reported back to Cole and Olley.

What a strange situation. A Chevrolet engineer drove race cars for Porsche. In addition, he had permission to exchange information to, and/or from, either side.

Duntov prepared a full report on the race for General Motors and access to that document provides some interesting comments. Duntov made the following observations arising from the practice sessions before the race: 1) Engine is completely devoid of life below 4000 rpm on the 1500cc car and below 4500 rpm on the 1100cc car; 2) First and second gear too low; 3) Transitional oversteer or extreme rapidity of response; 4) Steady state attainable only under moderate lateral accelerations; 5) Oversteer, breakaway with unmistakable tendency to swap ends at higher lateral acceleration; 6) Wind wander; and 7) The behavior is very much affected by the fuel content in the tank.

Much of the report pertains to the race and the following excerpts provide a historic perspective on that event:

"The race objective for Porsche was to achieve two class victories, therefore, it had to be driven against class competition without regard to overall placing."

The 1954 LeMans 24-hour race began on June 12th, and ended on June 13th. Again, from the Duntov interview:

"We started the race. This time, way back on the end of a starting grid, we displayed the agility hardly compatible with our age, and were one of the first underway. We drove for about 1.5 hours at a fast but strainless clip when the first pit signal to slow down appeared. It seemed irrational to ease off as we drove strainless already ... What we did not know was that a practice car was lost with an ailment the day before, and that one of the 1500cc Porsches was a victim of the same ailment after only four laps of racing and that after 1.5 hours, we had lapped all the 1100 class cars at least once.

"As I suspected, the driving of a less powerful car turned out to be a much easier task, mainly because on the undulated part of the circuit, the small car simply does not reach the speed at which the slight bends become difficult. With reserve in adhesion, the car is not as closely committed to the predetermined radius and gives the driver considerably leeway ...

"Unlikely as some organizations, which provide personnel with all the comforts, but have a sloppy pit, Porsche did not give a hoot about the drivers' or anybody else's comfort, but the managing of the race and the pits was excellent. We slept in reclining seats of Porsche passenger cars parked in the rear, none the worse for experience. Only two mechanics — engine and chassis — are assigned to each car. They are in readiness for 24 hours. They and other pit personnel had only cat naps without leaving their posts throughout the race ...

"The race continued uneventful until near the end of my third spell when after one of the torrential outbursts, the engine started to misfire and concurrently we found ourselves with a limp gear lever. Our heart skipped a beat, but we were acting too fast to have time to get really worried. We stopped and got the idea that the big tube running backwards from the lever is connected in some way to the transmission. We yanked it until it registered, drove off in reverse, yanked some more and were sputtering in high gear, but forward.

"The transmission trouble was corrected at the pit, but remained fragile and we used only three gears out of four. When shortly afterwards my co-driver took over, he was handling the transmission better and was using all four gears. The misfire was put down to cold oil which did not make sense, but with something like a 15-lap lead, we retired to sleep — essentially finished as far as driving was concerned.

"We were aroused with the order to get ready to take over. The lead dwindled to seven laps and we were losing 10 seconds per lap to Osca. Something over two hours remained in the race. With confidence in the automobile somewhat undermined, we were very apprehensive starting on this last leg ...

"The original field dwindled down from 58 to some 20 cars. We could not understand what held some 200,000 people under torrential rain around the circuit. For our part, we were concentrating on not getting in any trouble, particularly with the furious battling between the remaining Ferrari and Jaguar.

"The pit counters were lined with personnel and on each passage the manager motioned to take it easy. With some eight minutes to go, we entered which we decided to be our last lap, as there was not enough time to make two. However, driving slowly as to time the crossing of the finishing line with the end of the race (timed at 24 hours), we were passed by our 1500cc Porsche which motioned to line up parallel to cross the finishing line together. Our estimation must have been different as he was going at a livelier clip than I had planned.

"We crossed the finishing line a few seconds too early and had to make another lap. We did not regret this lap. The rain had stopped a while back, and for eight miles the clapping and cheering spectators were drowning the noise of the open exhaust.

"Then, after 24 hours and some minutes, we got our checkered flag. We won the class and were 14 overall (only 18 of 58 finished — also a record)."

After the race, Duntov was invited to Zuffenhausen where he spent a few days helping analyze the race and car performance. While there, he worked with eight racing engineers including Leopold Schmid, the chief engineer of Porsche. During the meetings he met an impressive young engineer named Helmut Bott who was forthright with his questions. The main topic was the twitchy driving characteristics of the Spyder at LeMans. Duntov provided Bott with materials from General Motors technical journals concerning the driving behavior of the automobile. The author was his boss, Maurice Olley of General Motors. Bott started to experiment with handling analysis on skid pads.

In separate meetings with Ferry Porsche, Duntov said that to improve the car, they would need stabilizer bars. He also said the engine needed about 30 additional horsepower.

Duntov returned to the U.S. after visiting other German companies. In August, he received a follow-up report from Porsche. In a memo dated September 27, 1954, he summarized by saying, "Received the preliminary test reports with suggested changes on Porsche cars together with additional related investigation." The main conclusions of the report were:

"1) Installation of stabilizer bars of 12mm resulted in higher maximum speed on turns and reduced tendency to oversteer. The stabilizer bars were immediately installed on all Porsche racing cars. Tests of 12, 13 and 14mm stabilizers are underway on standard cars and also on Volkswagen.

"2) Rear wheel toe-in in the range of 0-40mm has greater straight-ahead added stability. Preferred toe-in is 10mm. On turns, toe-in resulted in increased maximum speed and greatly reduced oversteering tendency.

"Front sway bars were mounted on the four 550s entered at the Nurrburgring race later in the summer. The bars were added by building a drop link off the bottom of the shock absorber. The modified cars were impressive, taking the first four places."

As we know now, Duntov's experience with suspension systems helped Porsche to install the correct size stabilizer bars on the front. As we see from Duntov's comments, the Porsche's handling was greatly improved. Later in Corvette production (1960), stabilizer bars were added on the rear of production Corvettes.

Norm Brown
interview

Based on a 1986 interview by Noland Adams

Chapter

11

Norm Brown's first day on the job was July 8, 1955. It would be a memorable day, as we shall see. Norm worked his way up in Chevrolet, specializing in building big block engines for folks like Jim Hall, Roger Penske, Corning Fiberglass and Tony DeLorenzo.

In 1980, Norm transferred to the desert proving grounds in Arizona. Norm still works in the engine and fuel injection development area.

Noland: "Describe your first day at work, which I understand was July 8, 1955. Is that correct?"

Norm: "That's correct. I had graduated from high school on a half-year basis in January, and I didn't get to 18 years of age until May. A friend of mine had already obtained a job with Chevrolet at the Engineering Center in Warren. Well, eventually, he was able to get me an application and I filled it out and they said I could start on July 8th on the afternoon shift. So I showed up for work on time, and as usual with a new guy, they were looking for something for me to do, so they said go with this mechanic over to the test car garage, and scrap some vehicles.

"When I got to the garage area, I saw that the vehicles we were going to scrap were show-type vehicles that were prevalent back in those days. One of those vehicles looked, at this point, like a miniature production Nomad — a '55 Chevrolet vehicle that I had seen, you know, a production vehicle, but this had a Corvette front end on it. The car that I was asked to scrap was, in fact, the original Corvette Nomad."

Noland: "Okay, how about the other car, do you remember anything about it?"

Norm: "Well, it's a long time ago — 31 years. I believe that car — I remember the Biscayne, and the vehicle was the Biscayne — but I can't tie together the dates particularly, although I did help scrap the Biscayne car, and I think it was on that same night that we did the Nomad, but I can't be positive on that. Also, sometime in this first period of time that I started working there the Impala was scrapped out also, although I didn't really see that vehicle or have anything to do with it."

Noland: "Okay, that settles the other car, we're not sure, but it could have been the Biscayne. What about the Nomad, what was its condition when you (first) saw it?"

Norm: "Well, the vehicle was still intact, and I don't remember whether it indeed had an engine or not, to be honest with you. Everybody there was really kind of blase and nonchalant about it — they said well, here are some Phillips head screwdrivers, some hammers, and whatever you need — start tearing this car apart so that we can indeed scrap it. So, how do you scrap it? They said well, take all the windshield molding out, we'll bust the windshield out of it, remove trim panels, anything that you can get off the car: headlight rims and headlights, and those sorts of things, and then they'll put it in a big crusher, and make it into a pile of dust, so to speak."

Noland: "You told me once that you got inside and removed all the trim, right?"

Norm: "Yeah, that's what I was eluding to — is they handed me a Phillips screwdriver, and said start taking all the pieces off that you can get off the car, so I started inside with the windshield moldings, anything that a Phillips screwdriver would fit at that point we took off, which was the side window moldings, and the rear window moldings, and tailgate window moldings, we removed the hubcaps — anything that was simple enough to get off — we just bent all these pieces up, threw 'em in a big trash barrel."

Noland: "You said it took you an hour or two to do all this?"

Norm: "Yeah, I think we worked on it probably a little longer than that, maybe until the lunch break which might have been two or three hours from the time I started because the first hour or so was kind of an orientation."

Noland: "That was both cars, huh?"

Norm: "Yeah, it didn't take us very long, because the way they scrap the vehicles essentially is in a crusher, but at this particular time — for whatever reason — they wanted all the trim pieces — anything that we could get off easily — door panels, door handles — those sort of things, were taken off and scrapped immediately. Now, the vehicle itself, after we finished with it, a group of material handlers came in and pushed the vehicle out. It was still on wheels, but they pushed it out and took it down to an area where it would be crushed the next working day, which I think was probably a Monday or so, based on dates back at that time."

Noland: "Looking at an old calendar, the next working day was Monday, July 11, (1955), so that was probably the day the shell of the body was crushed."

Norm: "Yeah, I don't imagine they did it on Saturday, because that would have been an overtime day, and I guess I don't really remember whether we worked overtime or not, but I'm pretty certain they wouldn't do that kind of a mundane task on an overtime day."

Well folks, now we know what happened to the Nomad. Well, not exactly. Norm wasn't there when the body was destroyed. Perhaps it survived, but the chances are small.

Major parts of the front end of the Biscayne dream car were found at a salvage yard north of the proving grounds. The Biscayne is in private hands, and it's being rebuilt. There are no remains of the Corvette Nomad, so who knows. It probably was broken in small pieces and scrapped. Still, it might exist somewhere.

The 1954 Chevrolet Corvette Nomad, which Norm Brown stripped in preparation for scrapping.

Cameo Carrier

General Motors was way out in front when it came to designing unusual dream cars. First, there had been the Corvette Nomad station wagon, shown at the 1954 Motorama.

The next was a dream car van, the L'Universalle, first shown in 1955.

The next surprise from the design group was a dream car-like design in a pickup. The unusual development of the Cameo Carrier was to bypass the dream car stage entirely. Suddenly, there was the Cameo Carrier, ready to buy at your nearest Chevrolet dealer.

The Cameo Carrier was a luxury version of a standard Chevrolet pickup. It sported a sleeker, smoother body, and it had a fancy interior.

But the main feature of the Cameo was the design of the rear exterior body. The standard metal pickup box was covered by smooth, fiberglass exterior panels. The tailgate had a fiberglass exterior with sleeker styling.

The Cameo Carrier was advertised — and sold — just like regular Chevrolet pickups. Cameos were made in 1955, 1956, 1957 and 1958. All had distinctive model-year styling, and all are considered collectible.

Chevrolet's Cameo Carrier was related to the Corvette. Its exterior bed panels and tailgate were fiberglass, both made by the Molded Fiberglass Company of Ashtabula, Ohio; the same folks who made most of the Corvette's body panels.

1955 design proposals

Chapter
13

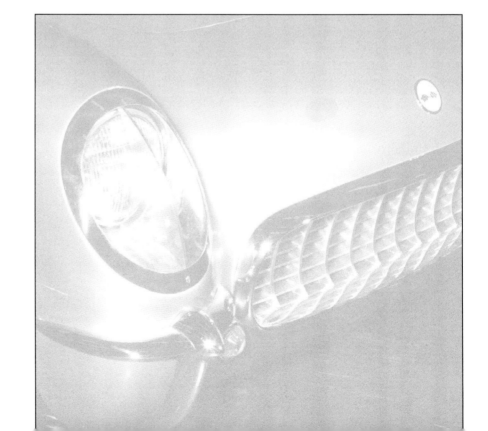

March 24, 1954; the Chevrolet design studios had been working on an improved design for the 1955 Corvette. A 1954 Corvette, serial number E545100, was provided to the design studios.

The vehicle was assigned shop order 2151, and a metal plate with "S.O. 2151" was riveted on the dash under the hood. It was fitted with a special concave grille, fabricated from many pieces of metal. The hood had a phony hood scoop, very much like the hood scoop on 1958 production Fords.

The side coves had four diagonal openings, each with its own chrome plated trim. This is very much like the 1965 and 1966 front fender side design, except: 1) '65 and '66 had three vents, 2) '65 and '66 had no trim around the openings, and 3) the '65 and '66 designs were vertical.

In the rear, the trunk lid had a raised top lid. From the rear, the design and trim on the raised area resembled the trunk treatment on the 1954 Corvette Corvair dream car.

S.O. 2151 was ready for presentation to upper management on March 24, 1954. After it was shown for consideration, S.O. 2151 disappeared. Not a single one of its proposed changes was used on the 1955 Corvette.

In 1983, the car surfaced on the used car lot of a Northern California Chevrolet dealer. It had seen a lot of use, for the body was in primer, which had cracked and was threatening to drop off in large chunks. It had a stock trunk and hood, and the grille was missing. The S.O. 2151 plate under the hood and the special trim on the front fender vents were still in place. Unfortunately, the dealer had no idea where the car came from and its history was lost.

Despite its being new, someone in the styling studio decided the 1955 Corvette needed a slightly different look. In January 1954 a new 1954 Corvette was brought into the 10th floor studios. When it came into the shop it was assigned a shop order number: S.O. 2151.

There were to be no major changes, just trim upgrades. The grille teeth were gone, replaced by a concave eggcrate grille.

On the front fender were four new vents, slanted toward the front, with a chrome trim outlining the vent.

The hood had a small non-functional scoop, much like the hood scoop on 1958 Ford passenger cars.

The trunk was large, with a flat area around the license plate mounting area. The trunk appeared to be identical to the trunk area on the 1954 Corvair dream car.

The car disappeared until it surfaced on a Chevrolet dealer's used car lot in 1982. The special hood, grille and trunk lid were missing. Perhaps they were changed to stock items before the car was sold.

However, a metal plate saying "S.O. 2151" and the date was riveted to the right side firewall, and cast right into the vent chrome trim. The car is now under restoration in private hands.

The 1955 proposal car, shown in these two shots, was photographed March 4, 1954.

EVANS
3-4-54

8497

Grille close-up taken March 24, 1954 shows a divider on the right headlight. This was an attempt to get away from the headlight screens, which were considered illegal by some states.

The close-up of the hood scoop.

From the rear, the modified exhaust outlets and trunk lid trim are unique.

The recessed rear license plate area.

The exhaust outlets have been relocated to the corners, which would be seen on 1956 production Corvettes.

The I.D. plate on the right side of the firewall shows when modifications to shop order 2151 were started: July 30, 1954.

The condition of S.O. 2151 when it resurfaced on a Chevy dealership's used car lot in 1982. The vent trim and long horizontal side trim were still with the car.

The rear of the car had been returned to near-stock condition.

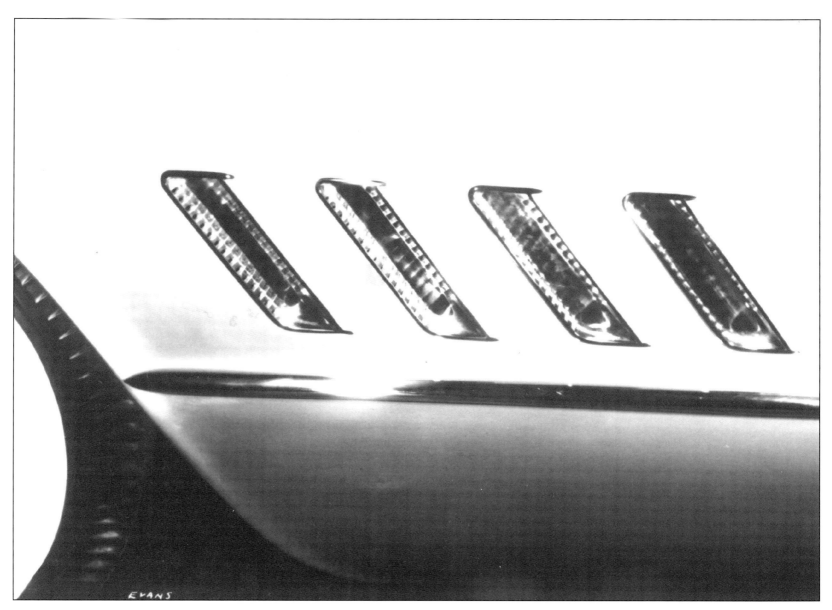

Here's a close-up of the side trim on the left fender.

1955 Corvette production begins

The 1955 Corvette V-8
looked just like a 1954
except for a big gold plated
"V" over the side trim.

Close-up of the gold
plated "V" over the
chrome plated script.

Production of the 1955 Corvette began in January of 1955. Even by Spring sales were poor; there was no cause for celebration.

Chevrolet had a large number of unsold 1954 Corvettes in dealers' showrooms or at the St. Louis assembly plant. Designed to produce 1,000 Corvettes each month, the assembly line was just getting up to full speed in June. Faced with decreasing sales, the assembly plant shipping lot was becoming a storage lot. The St. Louis Corvette plant was forced to cut back production to a fast crawl. Many workers were transferred to the nearby passenger car line or pickup line.

Since the 1955 Corvette assembly line was similar to the 1954 line, all the manufacturing processes were unchanged. Of course, the V-8 engine was new, but the lack of sales overshadowed that. There were no known photos taken of the 1955 assembly line.

The 1955 Corvette suffered from a lack of enthusiasm throughout Chevrolet. This was exhibited by employees at Chevrolet dealerships, further depressing sales.

This writer had purchased a used 1954 Corvette in April of 1955. By July, I wanted a new Corvette V-8, so I went to the largest Chevrolet dealer around — Helm Chevrolet in Modesto, Calif.

Helm Chevrolet had a large, busy showroom. They were selling new 1955 Power Pack Chevrolet V-8s as fast as they could get them. But — Corvette? The dealer had no information about the 1955 Corvette at all. They had to call the zone office to find out what colors and options were available. And finding out the retail price was really tough. It was like Helm was determined to avoid selling Corvettes.

In the end, it didn't matter. I owed too much on the '54 to make a deal. But even that made a bit of history. How many Corvette owners do you know who tried to trade in a year-old Corvette on a new 1955 Corvette?

Later, I was responsible for the sale of a new 1955 Corvette. In the summer of 1955, I hung around with a lot of car guys. One day I met a guy named Brian who lived in Stockton.

Brian had just completed some type of major accomplishment, and his parents were pleased. I can't recall what it was exactly, but he'd been accepted to college, or graduated from college — something like that.

Brian's father had promised him a new car. After a couple of rides in my '54, Brian was convinced. He immediately told his parents he wanted a new Corvette. Brian's mother had a classic reply: "Honey, we don't want you in one of those little European cars." Brian replied: "But mother, the Corvette is made by Chevrolet. Right here in America." His parents agreed on the spot to buy him a Corvette.

I didn't know about their decision to buy the Corvette until later. I would have surely liked to have been there. It seems Brian's father walked into Chase Chevrolet in Stockton, Calif. and announced he wanted to buy a Corvette. Cash. No dickering. I'll bet the salesman was shocked.

Under the hood was an all new 265-cid V-8 producing 195 hp.

The 1955 Corvette V-8 engine had a large air cleaner and chrome plated valve covers.

The ignition coil and distributor had special shielding which prevented electrical noise (static) from interfering with radio reception.

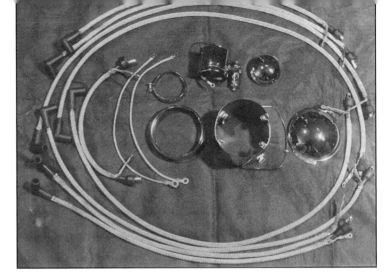

The complete set of ignition wiring includes shielded spark plug wires, the shielded coil-to-distributor wire, and two ground wires.

From this view we can see the shielding on the distributor, with the shielded spark plug wires coming out both sides. The coil (horizontal beside the brake master cylinder) is also shielded.

A 1955 Corvette is shown on display in a dealer's showroom.

End of
1955 production

The serial number plate from VE55S001001, not only the first 1955 Corvette, but the first V-8 engined production Corvette.

The serial number plate on VE55S001700, the 700th — and last — 1955 Corvette.

Looking back at 1955 Corvette production, we see a difficult year for General Motors and its Chevrolet Motor Division. Amid glowing testimonials, the Motorama Dream Car was rushed into production in 1953. New production facilities at St. Louis promised to increase production to meet public demand.

Yet 1954 Corvettes suffered slow sales. Many factors contributed; the Korean War had ended the year before. There had been a restriction on auto production. Some reports felt a changing economy left some folks uneasy.

The Chevrolet dealers attitude of "who needs a plastic-bodied two-seat sports car?" was a hindrance. The Corvette's lack of conveniences, especially when compared to Ford's new Thunderbird, turned people away. There were no organized clubs — nowhere to go to share your new Corvette with other enthusiasts.

These — and other factors — subdued 1954 Corvette sales. The St. Louis Corvette assembly line, designed to produce 50 units per day, idled along, barely running at all.

The beginning of 1955 production saw an overstock of 1954 Corvettes. The first order of business on the 1955 production line was to proceed slowly.

Sure the 1955 Corvette had the new 265-cid V-8 engine producing 195 horsepower. But early 1955 ads failed to emphasize the new V-8. In retrospect, the V-8 engine was new, and very few folks realized just how excellent it really was.

Chevrolet dealers, burdened with excess stock of 1954 Corvettes, weren't anxious to push 1955 Corvette sales. Potential Corvette purchasers — and enthusiastic Corvette salesmen — were both hard to find.

Let's look back at 1955 production:

Month	Last Serial No.	Units Per Month
January 1955	001027	27
February	001110	83
March	001150	40
April	001200	50
May	001300	100
June	001389	89
July	001489	100
August	001555	66
September	001599	44
October	001634	35
November	001688	54
December	001700	12

The December unit production number of 12 is understandable, since 1955 production ended early in the month, in preparation for the next model year's production.

But look at the monthly units produced. Even a high of 100 units could be turned out in two working days by an experienced, up-to-speed Corvette assembly line.

1955 Corvette production must have been an embarrassment for GM and Chevrolet upper management. Yet the challenge voiced by Zora Arkus-Duntov had been met head on. An improved Corvette, filled with convenience options, was planned for the 1956 model year.

While 1954 and 1955 model years were disappointments, the upcoming 1956 year was full of promise.

Unusual
1955 variations

During the early development days of the automobile, many different electrical systems were developed. By the forties, most cars used a six-volt system. However, some had a negative ground system; others used a positive ground system.

In the fifties, the automobile manufacturing companies agreed to standardize electrical systems. All 1954 Chevrolets utilized a six-volt negative-ground system. At the beginning of 1955 production, all GM cars changed over to a 12-volt negative-ground system.

On the surface, one could say 1954 Chevrolets had six-volt systems, and 1955 Chevrolets had 12-volt systems. That is how the electrical system change over was planned, but that's not what happened.

Due to poor sales, there were enough parts left over from 1954 production to assemble a few six-cylinder powered Corvettes in 1955. The exact number is unknown, but it's expected to be less than 10 units.

The 1955 six-cylinder powered Corvettes had several unique features. The engine code suffix which identified the engine as being assembled for a certain model year did state the year as "55". However, the suffix was scratched into the engine pad. All others — 1954 six-cylinder and 1955 eight-cylinder engine blocks — had their engine numbers stamped on, using metal dies.

Second, the regular 1955 Corvette was powered by a V-8 engine. This was reflected by the prefix "V" stamped on the serial number plate. Examples: VE55S001001 is from the V-8 powered #1. E55S001320 is from the six-cylinder powered #320.

The serial number plates on 1955 Corvettes with six-cylinder engines had no "V" prefix, like this plate from E55S001320.

The serial number plate on V-8 powered 1955 Corvettes had a "V" prefix. This plate is from VE55S001001, serial number one, the first V-8 powered production Corvette.

Third is the electrical system. All the devices that were matched to the six-cylinder engine used a six-volt, negative ground system. That meant the starter, generator, voltage regulator, radio, horn relay, and all light bulbs were six-volt units.

Now, we can chart these:

- 1950 to 1954 Chevrolets
  - six-volt system

- 1955 Corvettes with six-cylinder engines
  - six-volt system

- 1955 all, except 1955 six-cylinder Corvettes
  - 12-volt system

- 1956 and later
  - 12-volt system

This chart shows the availability of six or V-8 engines and the availability of colors.

CHEVROLET MOTOR DIVISION

CENTRAL MOTORS CORPORATION

DETROIT 28, MICHIGAN

8211 DECATUR AVENUE

March 25, 1955

Bulletin D-1982

Subject: New Colors and Trim for 1955 Corvette

TO ALL DEALERS:

During the month of April a new line of colors will be introduced on the Chevrolet Corvette - they are as follows:

RPO NUMBER	USED WITH	EXTERIOR	TRIM	TOP
Standard	6-or 8-cyl.	Polo White	Red	White
440K	6-cylinder	Harvest Gold	Yellow	Green
440L	8-cylinder	Harvest Gold	Yellow	Green
440M	6-cylinder	Gypsy Red	Beige (Light)	Beige
440N	8-cylinder	Gypsy Red	Beige (Light)	Beige
440P	6-cylinder	Bronze (Metallic)	Beige (Dark)	White
440Q	8-cylinder	Bronze (Metallic)	Beige (Dark)	White

All Corvette tops will now be fabricated out of a new vinyl-coated canvas material called Cotan.

While Pennant Blue is being discontinued April 1, Dealers should contact the Zone if they receive an order in this color since it is possible the plant may have a few unassigned Blue Corvettes in the yard for a short period of time.

The availability date probably will vary between the various new colors. Therefore, Dealers should contact the Zone on any order requiring early April delivery to determine the exact date trim will be available to produce that particular color.

Please advise all interested parties in your dealership.

Very truly yours,

L. L. Barr
k.

L. L. Barr
Distribution Manager

LLB/k

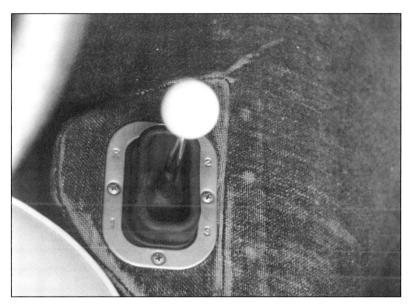

This first series of 1955 Corvettes equipped with three-speed transmissions used a flexible shifter boot without a shift pattern indicator.

The second type of 1955 three-speed shifter had a rectangular boot, retained by a stamped steel bezel.

Another unusual variation in 1955 was the transmission. When the Corvette was ordered into production after the 1953 Motorama, the only transmission available was the two-speed automatic Powerglide.

Chevrolet engineers were looking for a manual transmission for the 1953 Corvette. Chevrolet passenger cars had a three-speed manual transmission, which might be adapted to fit the Corvette.

After testing, it was decided the passenger car manual transmission was not strong enough. The engineers tried to improve the durability of the transmission by having the gears heat-treated. This heat treating process was not successful, leaving only Powerglide as the transmission for the Corvette.

Paperwork from that period is not clear about the problem in getting the transmission's gears properly heat treated. One must recall that the Korean War was going on at the time and there was a shortage of material, equipment and skilled manpower. Perhaps the Korean War was at least partially responsible.

Development work began on a new three-speed transmission. It was completed during mid-1955 production. The transmission was built by the Saginaw Division of General Motors.

The underside of the 1955 three-speed shifter shows how the shifter pattern is embossed in the bezel.

In order to test the three-speed transmission installation, a complete set-up was supplied to the St. Louis assembly line. The clutch, transmission, shifter, and linkages were installed in a production Corvette as soon as they arrived.

The 1955 three-speed transmission-equipped Corvettes were shipped to the GM proving ground. There they were adjusted, tested and modified as necessary. There were several prototypes built in the factory beginning at approximately mid-model year production. As soon as one had completed testing, a complete set of improved parts was sent to the St. Louis assembly plant. Then a Corvette was assembled using the improved three-speed and sent out for testing. After testing, the cars were wholesaled to nearby Chevrolet dealers as used cars. The units that only required adjustments or minor modifications were sent on to dealers as new units.

Only a few — maybe four or five — were made with the leather boot over the shifter shaft. The next version used a rubber-like rectangular boot (seal) to fill the gap around the shifter handle. A metal bezel was stamped out to retain the edges of the rubber seal. The location of the gears was stamped into the bezel, like R-1-2-3.

The metal bezel and the rubber seal system was used on several randomly selected 1955 Corvettes, about three-quarters of the way through the production run of 700. After the three-speed transmission and its other parts had proven themselves in random production line installations, all of the rest of 1955 Corvette production was equipped with three-speed transmissions.

Now the interior design group had to modify the shift lever area of the carpet to accommodate a new shifter design. The first three-speed shifter design was seen as a vertical shifter shaft rising from the carpet in the transmission tunnel area. (Powerglide-equipped Corvettes had a horizontal shaft with a vertical shifter shaft.) The shaft of the three-speed shifter was covered with leather or an imitation leather shift boot. This is very similar to some European cars. The gear shift was a plain knob; no sign of a shift pattern.

Dealer drive-aways: Pasadena, Chicago

Chapter

17

Twenty eight 1954 Corvettes are lined up at the Pasadena Rose Bowl for the Los Angeles dealers drive-away. Note that some cars have license plates, and all the drivers are wearing their dealer's shop coats.

Chevrolet wanted to get more information out on its 1954 Corvette. The sales areas throughout the U.S. were called "zones": most major cities had a zone office.

The plan was to bring in service personnel from all the dealers within a zone. They would meet at the General Motors Training Center (each zone had one). There would be classes on the Corvette — body and chassis servicing information. Then they would each get in a new Corvette, and drive it back to the dealership.

But the drive back to the dealership took some detours. The convoy of new Corvettes stopped at every photo opportunity.

The Corvettes themselves were special. Up until now, all Corvettes were white with red interiors. The assembly plant managers realized that cars with red interiors could also be painted red or black. The drive-away Corvettes were basically white, but with a good representation of red and black models.

Sales restrictions were being relaxed, and it was time to get the public interested in Corvettes. On March 17, 1954, dealer representatives met at the General Motors Training Center on Riverside Drive in San Fernando, just north of Los Angeles.

After hearing how wonderful the Corvette was, they each got a chance to drive one. The first stop was the parking lot of the Rose Bowl in Pasadena, Calif. Several photos were taken, then they drove south toward downtown Los Angeles.

The Harbor Freeway, a major mover of cars nowadays, was under construction in 1954. The Corvettes parked in neat rows while several photos were taken.

What happened: 1. Dealer personnel learned more about the Corvette; 2. Each person got to drive one; 3. Publicity photos were taken to be widely distributed; 4. Hopefully, this enthusiasm about the Corvette would rub off on the salesmen, and more Corvettes would be sold.

There was another unexpected event. Sometimes smaller dealers would send a service manager to the Corvette Drive-Away, but they didn't want the new Corvette. In those days Harry Mann was a major Chevrolet dealer. Harry Mann's general manager was Frank Milne, who agreed to take all the Corvettes other dealers didn't want. Chevrolet never forgot that, and sometimes Harry Mann Chevrolet got special considerations. For many years, Harry Mann sold more Corvettes than any other dealer.

The Corvettes drove south to the almost-completed but-not-yet-opened Harbor Freeway through Los Angeles. The four darkest cars were black, the other eight dark cars were red and the rest were white.

The Corvettes were parked on the Harbor Freeway — downtown Los Angeles is in the background.

Chicago-area dealers drive new Corvettes on Lakeshore Drive. Downtown Chicago is in the background.

On April 27, 1954 the Chicago area Chevrolet zone office staged another dealer driveaway. Representatives from Chevrolet dealers in the Chicago area met at the General Motors Training Center after being given a healthy dose of propaganda, they all drove away in new Corvettes.

The Corvette convoy was photographed on Lakeshore Drive with the Chicago skyline in the background. Of particular interest is the common passenger cars of the day in the opposite traffic lanes.

In late May or early June there was a drive-away for members of the automotive press. These lucky guys drove new 1954 Corvettes to the St. Louis Corvette assembly plant. There they were able to see the Corvette assembly line first hand.

This is the first time non-General Motors employees were allowed to observe the assembly line in operation. They weren't allowed to take photographs; instead they were each supplied with a full set of assembly line photographs.

General Ames' Corvette

Chapter

18

In 1953 Major General Lawrence C. Ames was a stock broker in San Francisco and also, as founder and first commanding officer of the Northern California Wing of the California Air National Guard, was chief of staff for air to the Adjutant General of the State of California. In October of that year he saw an ad for a new Chevrolet product and went to the Van Ness Avenue showroom to view the 1953 prototype Corvette which was on display in the Ernest Ingold dealership on a rotating platform with a barrier cord around it.

As he stood admiring the vehicle and thinking to himself that Chevrolet had finally come up with something that could appeal to aviation-type guys, he overheard a bystander demand something like, "How are you ever going to sell one of these if you won't even let people sit in it?" Upon hearing that, the General spoke up and said "I'll show you how! I'll buy one!" He wrote out a $100 deposit check on the spot.

The deposit was accepted by the dealership, but purchasing a new Corvette was more than just a matter of money. One had to be a person of importance; of proper stature. Your very presence behind the wheel of your new Corvette would cause the common folk to sit up and take notice. General Ames was, indeed, a "worthy" person with the proper credentials to purchase a new Corvette.

His military record reads like the history of aviation: Driver for the American Field Ambulance Service and for the

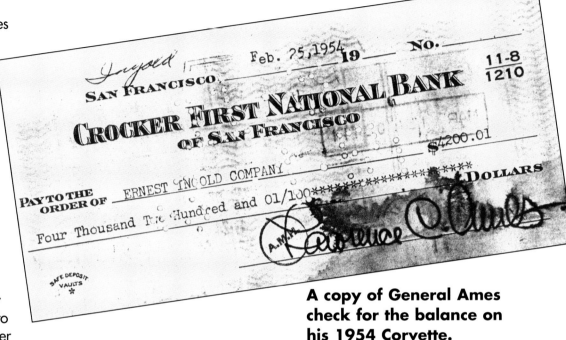

A copy of General Ames check for the balance on his 1954 Corvette.

American Red Cross, Cadet with the French Flying Corps and the Lafayette Escadrille, Lieutenant in the Air Services of the U.S. Army Signal Corps, Captain in the Army Air Corps Reserve, Major in the Army Industrial College, Lieutenant Colonel in the Western Procurement District buying aircraft for the U.S. Air Force, Colonel in the General Staff Corps in the Pentagon with service in both Iwo Jima and Germany, Brigadier General in the California Air National Guard and Major General in retirement after 1959 and during his years of government service as a member of the Reserve Forces Policy Board in Washington, D.C.

Although restrictions kept many Corvettes from being sold, they were in great demand for displays. This Corvette had been shown at the Portland Auto Show, then was brought to Corvallis, Ore. by the O'Toole Motor Company where it was placed on display at the Greater Corvallis Industry, Home and Farm Exposition from March 24 through March 28, 1954.

In order to get the Ernest Ingold Chevrolet dealership to sell him the car, General Ames had to prove that he was a SOME-BODY. No problem. General Curtis O'Sullivan may not be a name that is remembered now, but at that time he was the State's Adjutant General in charge of all the National Guard and Reserve Forces at the Governor's disposal. Letters from Governor Earl Warren and General O'Sullivan were able to help out when plain old Lawrence Ames needed recognition on Van Ness Avenue as a person "worthy" of owning a Corvette.

On the following February 25th he received one of the first Corvettes delivered by any dealer in Northern California. He showed off the car at the Pebble Beach Concours d'Elegance in June of 1954. In the following 16 years the Corvette became his trans-bay commute car. He sometimes drove the Corvette to Wyoming for the annual fly-in ranching party of the Conquistadors del Cielo, of which he was honored to be a member. He was the only stock broker welcomed into the ranks of all the CEOs of the major aircraft and airline companies of America. After 80,000 miles it was retired and put into mothballs for sentimental reasons.

The General died in 1981 at the age of 84, still a stock broker with his eyes in the air, into airline operations and into military flying, just as he had learned to do in both world wars and in private flying ventures and adventures in between the wars.

The Corvette has been shown at many NCC/NCRS events, but has never needed a body-off restoration, just periodic maintenance. The car is now owned by his son, Lawrence C. Ames, Jr., and someday his grandson, Lawrence C. Ames III, is going to be able to claim that he is the "original owner" of a 1954 Corvette even though he himself was not born until 1961.

The point of all this is to emphasize the restrictions on the sales of new Corvettes in early 1954. This procedure of requiring potential Corvette purchasers to prove they were "worthy" and "people of stature" continued until late in the spring of 1954, probably May. Imagine applying such standards to today's new Corvette buyers!

Corvette sales nosedive

Now that the Ford Thunderbird is a reality, let us examine the competition between the Thunderbird and the Chevrolet Corvette.

The Chevrolet Corvette had been designed as a dream car to be exhibited at the GM Motorama in New York City in mid-January 1953. All show cars at the time were called dream cars. Later they were called experimentals, one-offs, prototypes and/or concept cars.

The Chevrolet Corvette dream car built in 1952 was a running, fully functional car. However, it was built for indoor display, not to be used by the general public as an every day vehicle. In order to capitalize on the positive public reaction Chevrolet management expected, contingency production plans were made.

When the Corvette dream car was greeted by enthusiasm, the president of General Motors announced the car would be in production in less than six months. That meant the production Corvette of 1953 would use the same basic appointments as the Corvette dream car.

With a Chevrolet V-8 production engine two years away, a Chevrolet six-cylinder engine was modified to supply as much horsepower as possible. With only a Powerglide transmission available, it was beefed up to take the Corvette six's higher horsepower and torque. The body was slightly changed to allow the production of smaller panels which would be joined to produce the fiberglass body. It was so close to the Corvette Motorama car that advertisements shouted "The First of The Dream Cars To Come True." Therefore, the 1953 to 1955 production Corvettes were very similar to their dream car parent.

It was a major decision when the Chevrolet general sales manager decided to restrict sales of 1953 Corvettes to celebrities and folks in high visibility positions. This selected sales plan

for new Corvettes continued through 1953 over into the early Spring of 1954. By then, many would-be purchasers were tired of waiting, and went on to a more standard type of automobile. While potential Corvette buyers were waiting, Ford announced that its new Thunderbird would be available in the Fall.

And, the new Thunderbird would be loaded with features. For starters, the body would be metal, none of this mysterious plastic stuff. There would be roll-up safety glass windows with optional power lifts. The engine would be an overhead valve V-8 of the latest design. There would be a choice of transmissions. Other options included power seats and a removable snug-fitting hardtop.

Many who wanted to buy the Corvette and had been placed on a waiting list were having second thoughts. Instead of getting a crude car that looked like a dream car, they could wait and get a freshly designed, similarly sized car that was loaded with conveniences.

It worked. Chevrolet was now ready to sell 1954 Corvettes to the general public without restrictions, but there were few buyers. Inventories of unsold Corvettes backed up at Chevrolet dealers, and at the shipping lot at the Corvette assembly plant in St. Louis. By June of 1954, Corvette production had increased to 50 units per day. But with growing inventories of unsold Corvettes, the assembly line was closed for weeks at a time.

Another important detail that added to the slow Corvette sales was the attitude of the typical Chevrolet dealer. These dealers had been selling a lot of conservative, dependable six-cylinder sedans and trucks. Now the dealer was being supplied with a plastic-bodied, two-passenger sports car. The dealer's attitude was "Who needs it?"

The material of the body created a lot of questions, most with unknown answers. What happens in an accident? Can the plastic body be repaired? How much does body repair cost? Can the Corvette be repaired mechanically by every Chevrolet dealer? Does insurance cost more? These are the types of questions the salesmen had to answer, and most were unprepared to give a proper answer.

The dealers responded as one would expect. Some chose to promote and sell the Corvette. Other dealers chose to ignore it. In order to learn how to repair the plastic body, larger Chevrolet dealers sent one body man to school to learn how to repair the body. It really didn't help buyer confidence to have the salesman state "Yes, the body can be easily repaired. In fact, 'Bob' from the body shop went to a special school to learn how to fix it."

In the summer of 1955, this writer drove his 1954 Corvette into an active Chevrolet dealer (15 miles) to trade in the old '54 Corvette on a new V-8 powered Corvette. The dealer had no information at all; no brochure, nothing. They had to call the zone office to find out 1) what the car looked like; 2) what engine and transmission were available, 3) what colors the '55 Corvette came in, and 4) the cost. I went away disappointed because the dealer simply wasn't interested in selling a new Corvette.

Back in my hometown, the Chevrolet dealer didn't want to be bothered. The first Corvette it sold was a 1958 model, because the son of a local building contractor demanded one. In the meantime, the Ford dealership in my little town had three or four 1955 Thunderbirds in stock at all times during the summer of 1955. As a result, they sold a lot of Thunderbirds.

We're not done with the way the Ford Thunderbird influenced Chevrolet Corvette production. We'll pick up the rest of the story later in this book.

There were lots of other influences that shaped the Corvette.

Nowadays anyone buying a new or used Corvette acquires unlimited bragging rights. You are expected to drive over to all your friends, who will eyeball your new family member. Such friends are expected to oooh and aahh, and make you feel good.

But in 1954 anyone buying a Corvette was on his own. There were no clubs where you could meet folks with similar cars. There was no friend across town that had a Corvette. In fact, chances are, you had the only Corvette in your town.

In 1954, Corvette had no racing history. Nowadays Corvette's racing successes are well known and appreciated. Back in 1954, Corvette owners had no racing bragging rights, and the future of Corvettes was uncertain.

There were some ads, but they did little to stimulate Corvette interest and sales. If you were considering buying a Corvette, you walked into enemy territory (the new car sales department of a car dealership). Boy, those salesmen were intimidating. But if you were serious, you could actually buy a new car. You had to be really determined to buy a Corvette. Chances are you got a salesman who barely knew what a Corvette was, and he probably tried to talk you into the "nice Bel Air on the floor."

When one considers all the problems a potential Corvette owner faced, it's surprising that any 1954 Corvettes were sold at all.

Duntov's
challenge letter October 15, 1954

Chapter
20

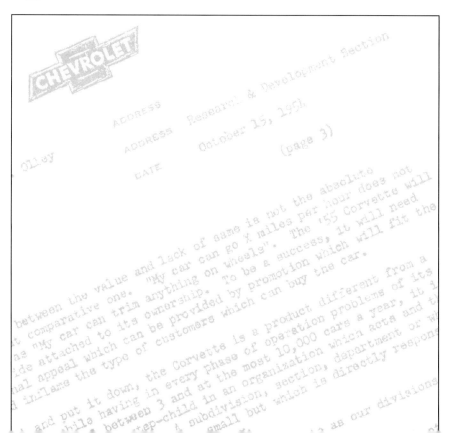

By October of 1954, Zora Arkus-Duntov was still an assistant staff engineer. He had worked for Chevrolet nearly 1-1/2 years, and he had earned a respect for his mechanical knowledge.

Even this early in his career Duntov had developed an affection for the Corvette. He observed the decrease in sales as the public reacted to the fiberglass body, Powerglide transmission, and lack of regular conveniences like roll-up windows. Corvette sales were — at best — slow.

Meanwhile, the threat from Ford's Thunderbird was growing. Now that production had begun, many potential Corvette buyers were waiting. Reports from the automotive press were glowing in their admiration for the Thunderbird's conveniences.

So Duntov took a hard, long look at the situation, and wrote the following letter:

Page 1 of letter

TO   Messrs. E. N. Cole and M. Olley   ADDRESS

FROM   Mr. Z. Arkus-Duntov   ADDRESS   Research & Development Section

SUBJECT CORVETTE   DATE   October 15, 1954

In this note I am speaking out of turn. I am giving opinions and suggestions without knowing all the factors. I realize this but still am offering my thoughts for what they are. In order to make the content clear and short, I will not use the polite apologetic phrasing and say, "it is" instead of "it possibly might be" - and I apologize for this now.

By the looks of it, the Corvette is on its way out.

I would like to say the following: Dropping the car now will have adverse effect internally and externally.

It is admission of failure. Failure of aggressive thinking in the eyes of the organization, failure to develop a saleable product in the eyes of the outside world.

Above-said can be dismissed as sentimentality, ~~let's see if it can hurt the cash register~~ but hurt our standing. I think it can.

Ford enters the field with the Thunderbird, a car of the same class as the Corvette.

If Ford makes success where we failed, it may hurt./

With aggressiveness of Ford publicity, they may turn the fact to their advantage. I don't mean in terms of Thunderbird sales, but in terms of promotion of theirs and depreciation of our general lines.

We will leave an opening in which they can hit at will. "Ford out-engineered, outsold, or ran Chevrolet's pride and joy off the market". Maybe the idea is far-fetched. I can only gauge in terms of my own reactions or actions. In the bare-fisted fight we are in now, I would hit at any opening I could find, and the situation where Ford enters and where Chevrolet retreats, it is not an opening, it is a hole!

Now if they can hurt us, then we can hurt them! We are one year ahead and we possibly learned some lessons which Ford has yet to learn.

Is the effort worthwhile? This, I am in no position to say. Obviously, in terms of direct sales a car for the discriminating low volume market is hardly an efficient investment of efforts. The value must be gauged by effects it may have on an overall picture.

Letter

Well now, folks, how about that challenge from a respected Chevrolet employee to keep the Corvette alive. There are no known records that tell us how the upper management at Chevrolet accepted Duntov's comments. However, we do know that the Corvette was saved, just as Duntov suggested.

If you like Corvettes, you'd just got to like Duntov. His letter helped to salvage the Corvette program.

Page 2 of letter

TO   Messrs. E. N. Cole and M. Olley   ADDRESS

FROM Mr. Z. Arkus-Duntov   ADDRESS Research & Development Section

SUBJECT CORVETTE   DATE   October 15, 1954

(page 2)

The Corvette failed because it did not meet G. M. standards of a product. It did not have the value for the money.

If the value of a car consists of practical values and emotional appeal, the sports car has very little of the first and consequently has to have an exaggerated amount of the second. If a passenger car must have an appeal, nothing short of a mating call will extract $4,000 for a small two-seater. The Corvette as it was offered had curtailed practical value being a poor performer. With a 6-cylinder engine, it was no better than the medium priced family car.

Timing was also unfortunate. When the novelty appeal was the highest, we hadn't had the cars to sell. When the cars became available, hypnotized by the initial overwhelming response, no promotional effort was made.

The little promotion which was made was designed to depreciate the car rather than enhance it. Hundreds or possibly thousands of dollars contained in the price of a sports or luxury car are paid for exclusivity. What did our promotion say on the radio and advertised in magazines? "Now everybody can have one. Come and get it". What virtues did advertising extoll? Only X inches high, only X inches long, etc. In the country, in which bigger is synonomous with better, and we really know it, we were trying to sell a car, because it is small! Crosley is smaller........

Were there no virtues to talk about? Quite some, but a condensation of test reports which appeared in motoring press previously had more glow and enthusiasm than our advertising.

Summarizing, the promotion was uninspired and half hearted attempt with no evidence of thought or enthusiasm.

Where do we stand now?

The Corvette still has the best and raciest look of all the sports cars, the Thunderbird included. Performance is far superior to all the passenger cars and to 99% of the sports cars used on the road. It has flow in respect to passenger protection. Water leaks and cumbersome top and side window. With these minor flaws removed, we have a sports car with as much practical value as the sports car can have.

TO   Messrs. E. N. Cole & M. Olley   ADDRESS

FROM   Mr. Z. Arkus-Duntov.   ADDRESS   Research & Development Section

SUBJECT   <u>CORVETTE</u>   DATE   October 15, 1954

(page 3)

The borderline between the value and lack of same is not the absolute performance but comparative one. "My car can go X miles per hour does not mean as much as "My car can trim anything on wheels". The '55 Corvette will have this pride attached to its ownership. To be a success, it will need more emotional appeal which can be provided by promotion which will fit the product and inflame the type of customers which can buy the car.

As I see it and put it down, the Corvette is a product different from a passenger automobile having in every phase of operation problems of its own. With sales potential between 3 and at the most 10,000 cars a year, it is bound to be a bindering step-child in an organization which acts and thinks in terms of 1,500,000 units. A subdivision, section, department or what not, but an organization no matter how small but which is directly responsible for the successes of operation is necessary.

An organization which will eat and sleep Corvette as our divisions are eating and sleeping their particular cars.

I am convinced that a group with concentrated objective will not only stand a chance to achieve the desired result, but devise ways and means to make the operation profitable in a direct business sense.

Z. Arkus-Duntov

ZAD:hs

Page 3
of letter

The challenge is accepted

Chapter

21

CORVETTE: AMERICAN LEGEND

The year 1954 had been a disappointing sales year for Corvette. Subdued Corvette sales continued into 1955, and the future of Corvette looked bleak, indeed.

Surely the future of the Corvette had been in doubt since June of 1954. Just as Corvette production approached the maximum planned output, slow sales caused a production cutback.

Upper management had to have second thoughts about continuing Corvette production. At the time, Corvettes had an unusual role. The presence of a Corvette brought new traffic into the Chevrolet dealer's showroom; an attraction that brought in folks who bought passenger cars and trucks.

The growing inventory of unsold Corvettes was becoming a concern. About that time — in October of 1954 — Chevrolet engineer Zora Arkus-Duntov wrote his Corvette Challenge Letter. If the possible cancellation of the Corvette was being kept quiet, the Duntov Challenge Letter brought the future of the Corvette out for open discussion.

Sometime in early 1955, GM upper management must have considered the future of the Corvette. Fortunately for Corvette enthusiasts, the GM response to the Thunderbird challenge was "Hey, you can't do that to us!" So Corvette production continued.

By March of 1955, the full-sized 1953 clay model had been reworked into a 1956 clay model. The 1956 Corvette was approved for production, and planned to meet the challenge of the Ford Thunderbird. We'll save the rest of this story for the 1956 book.

The 1953 full sized clay is being reworked into the improved 1956 model.

The first
export Corvette

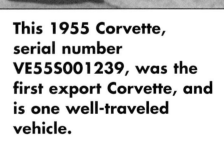

Vehicles are exported to other countries on a regular basis. The first known export Corvette was serial number VE55F001239, manufactured in mid-April 1955.

The car was shipped to Belgium. A metal plate is riveted to the right inner fender panel, which is stamped "General Motors Continental Antwerp."

Make   Chevy

Model: 2934

Engine: 0215625F55FG

Chassis: VE55F001239

and other information including:

Paint: White

Trim: Red

Year: 1955

This 1955 Corvette, serial number VE55S001239, was the first export Corvette, and is one well-traveled vehicle.

The "General Motors Continental" tag on the right inner fender panel.

The European radiator cap says "close tightly" and "open slowly" in German.

The spare tire was tubeless, yet it had a tube marked "Made in Holland."

The original owner is unknown. It had several owners in Belgium, France and Germany. In 1977, it was purchased by a member of the Canadian Armed Forces. In 1980, he shipped it back to Canada, where it was sold again in 1987 to another Canadian. In 1993, he brought it to Carlisle, where it was purchased by its current owner.

In 1993, for the first time, it had a U.S. owner.

Among its unique features is the metal plate mentioned before. The radiator cap is in German, stating "close tightly" and "open slowly."

Underneath the radio there is a decal placed there by Antwerp authorities. The spare tire contained a tube made in Holland.

As the first export model, this is a unique Corvette, indeed.

Joe Pike

Chapter

23

A new 1954 Corvette in the front window display at Frant Dover Chevrolet in Wilmington, Del.
(From the collection of Neil A. Blanchette)

Joe Pike began his career as an employee of Chevrolet in 1945. He was employed in the Minneapolis zone office in 1954, when a 1954 Corvette became available. Joe Pike purchased the car and became one of its biggest boosters.

Here is how Joe Pike explained it: "I purchased my first Corvette, a 1954 model, on Good Friday, April, 1954 from a small dealer in Wisconsin, whose VIP customer got tired of waiting for it and left for Honolulu. I drove the car 15,000 miles in the following four months, which included a trip down the Columbia River, down through Route 101 and back through Lake Tahoe and Yellowstone Park. After this experience I was completely 'hooked' and as a result I changed my entire career with Chevrolet.

Indeed, Joe Pike's career with Chevrolet did change. In 1956, he was transferred to Denver as regional organization manager. Pike was founder of the National

Council of Corvette Clubs. He encouraged Chevrolet dealers to stock parts and service Corvettes.

In 1959, Ed Cole, general manager of the Chevrolet Motor Division, visited Denver. Joe Pike was his driver. Ed Cole was so impressed by Pike that he suggested that Pike move to Detroit to serve as assistant national sales promotion manager in charge of Corvette production. As a result — but wait, I'm getting ahead of the story. We'll return to the Joe Pike story in a later volume.

The whole point about this story of Joe Pike's introduction to the Corvette is to illustrate the restricted sales of the Corvette. Later, Pike was to enjoy a reputation as the national spokesman for the Chevrolet Corvette. Yet, in April of 1954, as an employee of the Minneapolis Chevrolet Zone office, he was able to purchase a Corvette only when the original VIP purchaser was no longer interested.

The bottom line is — the sales of new Corvettes was restricted to "worthy" folks in April 1954. Records and magazine articles indicate Corvette sales were restricted through May. However, Chevrolet dealers were beginning to sell Corvettes to the general public. For the first time, mere money was enough to buy a new 1954 Corvette.

Outside view of front window display at Frant Dover Chevrolet.

The Ford factor

had always heard that the Ford engineers were seen measuring the prototype Corvette at the GM Motorama in January 1953. I had always assumed that that was the beginning of the Ford Thunderbird. And I had always known Corvette sales dropped in 1954 and 1955. It is generally understood that the Ford Thunderbird was directly responsible. In return, Chevrolet had reacted by producing an improved Corvette for 1956 in response to the challenge from Ford. The real story includes these rumors and partial facts, and much more.

Just as Harley Earl had envisioned a GM sports car in 1951, there was a group within Ford that envisioned a Ford sports car in the fall of 1951. The general manager of the Ford Division of the Ford Motor Company always attended the Paris Auto Show, a showcase for new models. We don't know what he saw, but in October of 1951 he called back to the Ford design group with instructions to begin designing a Ford sports car. During 1952, Ford's sports car project progressed at a slow rate because it was not included in the original budget. Thus, work was done

"on the side"; it progressed slowly because it was unofficial and undermanned with a low priority.

During 1952, Chevrolet was developing a prototype of the GM sports car (later called the Opel, then Corvette). It was built in the fall and winter of 1952 for introduction at the 1953 GM Motorama in January.

Ford's sports car program had produced several drawings and renderings by the fall of 1952. They obtained a preliminary drawing or photo of the GM sports car, which was called Project Opel

By 1952, the Ford sports car program had produced this full-sized drawing mounted on a piece of plywood.

By early 1953 several full-size drawings were under consideration.

at the time. Later, when the GM prototype, now called the Chevrolet Corvette, was shown at the GM Motorama in New York in mid-January 1953, Ford's engineers were on hand to check its dimensions.

Ford's engineers had also checked the dimensions of other potential competitors to their sports car program. The Nash-Healey, Chevrolet Corvette, and Kaiser Darrin 161 were all compared to their Ford sports car. Although they were all the same approximate size, only the Corvette survived to be compared directly to the Ford sports car. The Nash-Healey was produced in small quantities, and the Kaiser Darrin 161 ceased production in mid-1954.

The Ford sports car program got its official start in February of 1953. An internal product letter announced plans to build a two-seat sports car. This was a few weeks after the prototype Corvette was shown to the public for the first time. With increased support from upper management, the Ford sports car design began producing results. Did the Corvette prototype stimulate development of the Ford sports car program? It would seem so.

The Ford sports car was taking shape in the spring of 1953: this is a full-sized clay model.

The Ford group was confident that its yet-to-be-designed sports car would show well against the products from other manufacturers. It was to go "one-up" on the competition (Corvette and the Kaiser Darrin 161) by incorporating a steel body, a V-8 engine with choices of transmissions, and convenience and comfort features like roll-up windows.

Through the spring and summer of 1953, work on the Ford sports car was

In the summer of 1953, this clay model carried a bulge in its rear fender for tire clearance.

October, 1953: A 1953 Corvette on display at the Paris Auto Show. The front license reads "GM France."

progressing on several renderings and full-size clays. Renderings are shaded drawings which show dimensional details. Full-sized clays are sheets or lumps of clay spread over a wood framework (called an armature). The clay is shaped by hand to the car's general contours, then smoothed to produce the final shape. The clay can even be covered with a sheet of plastic, which is painted and trimmed like the real car. The result is amazing, for it looks just like a real car. The best hint is to look at the windows; if you cannot see through them, you may be looking at a full-sized clay.

By October 1953, several full-sized clays were finished, but the final shape hadn't been decided. Besides the clays of the original two-seat sports car, drawings of another version were started.

The general manager of the Ford division always attended the Paris Auto Show held in October of each year. Several other Ford executives went along to the 1953 Paris Auto Show in October, where a 1953 production Corvette was on display.

February 17, 1954: The fiberglass-bodied prototype is ready for the Detroit Auto Show. Note the rear fender has no emblem, but the gas cap lid has crossed flags and the name "Fairlane."

We don't know the Ford executive's exact thoughts, but we know part of what he saw: the 1953 Corvette. One of the Ford design group's managers immediately called the Ford studios in Michigan with directions to concentrate on the original version of the Ford sports car. This was the equivalent of a yellow caution light turning green. Thus the Corvette stimulated and influenced the Ford sports car program in October of 1953.

With full approval of upper management, the Ford sports car program shifted into high gear. A single prototype was prepared for presentation in early 1954.

One of the problems of the early Ford sports car program was storage of the folding convertible top. Some engineers wanted a top that was removed like a hardtop. Finally a top was designed that folded down into a compartment behind the seats, covered by a body panel.

By February the exterior details — including the folding top cover panel — had been decided. With the Detroit Auto Show only days away, all the final design details were incorporated into a single full-sized clay. Then a non-functional full-sized, fiberglass-bodied car was built.

The Detroit Auto Show opened with a special preview for members of the automotive press on February 17, 1954. Ford's

February 17, 1954: The Ford prototype is shown to members of the automotive press.

February 19, 1954: Ford press release lists T-Bird's good points.

sports car was on display, and it was well received by members of the press. From the June 1954 issue of *Motor Trend*: "experts who forecast that the Thunderbird would seem stark beside a Corvette are pleasantly surprised by its luxury."

The Detroit auto show version of the Ford sports car looked very much like the production car to follow in September. There were to be minor trim changes, but the basic design had been decided. However, the car did not yet have an official name. The name "Fairlane" was borrowed from Henry Ford's estate in Dearborn, Mich. named "Fair Lane." While the sports car by

Ford didn't have an official name before, it was finally known as the Fairlane during February of 1954.

The Detroit Auto Show ran for several days, with February 20, 1954 being the biggest day of the show. Public reaction to the "Fairlane" prototype was favorable with plenty of enthusiasm. This convinced Ford's engineers that they were on the right track. Plans for production were finalized; it would begin in the fall.

There had been a contest among Ford employees, to name the new car and the winner — Thunderbird — would represent the Ford sports car. While the "Fairlane" was on display, the name Thunderbird was announced in a news bulletin (left) dated February 19, 1954.

BULLETIN

Note that the hardtop is made from a "special composition." In reality, it was made from fiberglass. But, of course, Ford couldn't admit that, for that was the Corvette's body material.

March 25, 1954

Mr. ▧▧▧▧▧▧▧
▧▧▧▧▧▧▧▧▧
Los Angeles, California

Dear Sir:

Because of your interest in cars, both old and new, we thought you might be especially interested in some detailed information on the new Ford Thunderbird. The attached brochure outlines many of the unique features of our new sports car.

As you probably have heard, the Thunderbird was premiered at the Detroit Auto Show in February. It is scheduled for production this coming Fall.

In the event that you might desire additional copies of the brochure, we will be more than happy to send them to you.

Yours very truly,

F. J. McGinnis
Assistant General Sales Manager

Att.

March 25, 1954 - The letter that was sent out to all prospective purchasers with the first Thunderbird brochure.

T-Bird brochure, March 25, 1954

By March 1954, the Ford Sport Car program was fully funded and staffed. Members of the automotive press were pleased with the features of the prototype Fairlane they had seen at the Detroit Auto Show in February.

The folks at Ford didn't waste any time. In a company employee contest, the Ford Sports Car was renamed "Thunderbird."

It was important to get information out to the public, so a brochure was prepared. There wasn't time to wait for photographs, so hand drawn illustrations were used.

On March 25, 1954 a small package was mailed to thousands of potential Thunderbird purchasers. It contained two items: 1) a letter introducing the Ford Thunderbird, and 2) a brochure illustrating the features of the Thunderbird.

Drawings in the new brochure illustrated the folding soft top, and the removable hardtop, and the caption stated ".. An Exclusive Thunderbird feature!" Of course this was true, because these features were not available on either the Corvette or the Kaiser Darrin 161.

Another drawing showed the top down with the window rolled up. The caption emphasized the "Safety-Glass roll-up side windows" with "Power-lift Windows (are) available at extra cost."

The Thunderbird publicity campaign from Ford had begun!

built-in comfort and convenience!

SNUG COMFORT FOR ALL CLIMATES

To suit your personal car both to the seasons and to your tastes, there are two interchangeable tops . . . *an exclusive Thunderbird feature!* A smart, snug-fitting fabric top is built into the car, like a regular convertible. This top has a very large rear window for all-around visibility. And if you wish, you can have a handsome glass-fibre hard top that is color-matched to the car's body finish. This smartly finished top can be put on or removed with ease.

SAFETY-GLASS ROLL-UP SIDE WINDOWS

There is no need to sacrifice comfort for smartness in the Thunderbird. The all-glass side windows are the wind-up type and may be adjusted as easily as the windows in a sedan. Power-Lift Windows are available at extra cost.

CUSTOM-HARMONIZED INTERIORS

The interior of the Thunderbird is skilfully designed to reflect the distinctive beauty of the exterior lines. The big seat has more than enough room for two. And it's built for comfort . . . with thick foam-rubber cushions over super-resilient springs. A variety of smart upholstery patterns is available to harmonize perfectly with the beautiful body colors.

The first Thunderbird brochure emphasized its convenient features, features that the Corvette did not have.

The steering wheel telescopes a full 3 inches! And there's a 4-Way power-operated seat, too!

Luxurious, vinyl upholstery harmonizes with the color scheme of the car.

Recessed, push-button door handles are a great convenience.

The light, molded, glass-fibre top can easily be lifted on. It's beautifully lined and sound-insulated.

And if you want other custom conveniences like power steering, power brakes, power windows, Fordomatic or Overdrive ... they're all available for your Thunderbird.

THUNDERBIRD
SPECIFICATIONS:

Y-block V-8 Engine: Overhead valve, 90° V-type, 4-barrel carburetor; automatic choke; dual exhaust system; 3-ring superfitted aluminum alloy pistons. Free turning intake and exhaust valves. Pressure-type cooling system; full pressure lubrication. Six volt electrical system; weatherproof ignition, special 18mm plugs; 40-amp generator, 17-plate 90 amp-hr battery.

Semi-Centrifugal Type Clutch (except Fordomatic): dry, single plate type, 11 in. dia.; 113.1 sq. in. facing area; suspended pedal.

Conventional Drive: 3 speed type, all helical gears, floor-mounted lever. Ratios: low, 2.32 to 1; 2nd, 1.48 to 1; reverse, 2.82 to 1.

Overdrive: 3-speed transmission with planetary gear train providing automatic 4th gear. Manual lock-out. 4th gear ratio, 0.70 to 1.

Fordomatic: Single stage. 3 element torque converter; air cooled; automatic intermediate gear; automatic "low speed" starts with wide-open throttle; illuminated floor-mounted Safety Sequence selector lever.

Hotchkiss Drive: Tubular propeller shaft; needle bearings in universal joints; pressure type lubrication fittings.

Ball-Joint Front Suspension: Tailored to weight coil springs; ride stabilizer; double-acting shock absorbers.

Rear Suspension: Composite type axle housing; 5 leaf springs with inserts at tips of all leaves; double-acting shock absorbers; wind-up bumpers; tension-type rear shackles. Ratios 4.11 to 1 with Conventional; three 3.92 to 1 with Overdrive; and 3.30 to 1 with Fordomatic.

Frame: New low slung X type frame; box section side rails.

Brakes: 11" dia., double sealed, duo-servo type; 175 sq. in. lining area; suspended pedal.

Steering System: Symmetrical linkage type; 17" dia. wheel; 1" in-out adjustment; over all ratio 20 to 1; turning diameter, approx. 36 ft. (center of outside front tire).

Wheels and Tires: 6.70 x 15; 4-ply tubeless tires on 5" rims.

Exterior Dimensions: 102" wheelbase; 56" front and rear treads; 175.3" length; 70.3" width. Height with design load: 52.2" top of glass-fibre top to ground; 34.7" top of door to ground.

Interior Dimensions: 45.4" leg room; 58.8" hip room; 53.3" shoulder room; 33.2" head room (glass-fibre top). Trunk dimensions (max.): 58.2" width; 34.8" length; 18.1" height.

Color and Upholstery: Raven Black, Torch Red or Thunderbird Blue exterior body colors, with harmonizing Black and pleated White, Red and pleated White or Thunderbird Blue and pleated White vinyl interiors.

Other Features: Astra-Dial Control Panel with illuminated control knobs for main light switch, air ducts, windshield wipers; parcel compartment with locking-type push-button latch. 4-way illuminated starter ignition switch, steering tight in panel at center; supported by integral switch and automatic door catches. Rear view mirror on windshield upper molding. Dual horns; half-circle horn ring.

Available Equipment: Fuel flow oil filter; oil bath air cleaner; 4-Way Power Seat; Swift Sure Power Brakes; Master-Guide Power Steering; Power-Lift Windows; I-REST tinted safety glass; Fordomatic; Overdrive; white sidewall tires; tachometer; electric clock; cigarette lighter; glass-fibre top; convertible fabric top; special fuel and vacuum pump unit; heater; radio; rear fender shields; full wheel covers; simulated wire wheels; engine dress-up kit.

PRICES: Some of the items illustrated or referred to in this catalog are at extra cost. For the price of the Thunderbird with the equipment you desire, see your Ford Dealer.

The specifications contained herein were in effect at the time this folder was approved for printing. The Ford Division of the Ford Motor Company reserves the right to discontinue models at any time, or change specifications or design, without notice and without incurring obligation.

The 1955 Thunderbird in its final form. Angled louvers on the front fender are next to a horizontal seam that runs toward the rear. The nameplate "Thunderbird" is seen on the rear fenders.

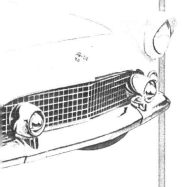

You can drive your Thunderbird with assurance, wherever you may go.

Though the Thunderbird is distinctively different, it is so engineered and built that it can be serviced by Ford Dealers - everywhere.

During the summer of 1954 work continued on 1955 Thunderbird variations. Here is an unusual front fender and body side trim, which never reached production.

The folding top in its upright position on the Thunderbird with unusual non-production side trim.

Thunderbird production begins - Sept. 1954

The first production Ford Thunderbird, a 1955 model, was assembled on Sept. 9, 1954. Thunderbird bodies were built by the Budd Company from Philadelphia. The Budd Company had experience building bodies for railroad cars and other automobiles. Budd built a Thunderbird body plant in East Detroit, and shipped the bodies to the Ford assembly plant at River Rouge.

At the Rouge Plant the Thunderbird bodies were trimmed on the second floor. Then the bodies were dropped to the first floor where they were assembled to their chassis along with standard sized 1955 Fords.

The body drop of a 1955 Thunderbird illustrates the start of production: September 9, 1954.

The Thunderbird goes on sale

The 1955 Ford Thunderbird was first shown in Ford dealer showrooms on Oct. 22, 1954. After all the advance publicity touting the car's features, the car was an instant success.

Chevrolet's advertising pointed out that the Thunderbird was nothing more than a downsized Ford convertible. That was true to a point, but the Thunderbird was quite different from the full sized convertible. It had its own identity; unique body style and trim, plus it held only two people. A third person could sit in the middle, but there was very little padding on the transmission tunnel, making the center person squirm on long trips.

The metal body, the V-8 engine, plus all the convenience features, made the car an instant hit. There were 4,000 orders taken that first day, Oct. 22nd.

At this time, Ford was still calling the Thunderbird a sports car. An article in the December 1954 issue of *Motor Trend* stated that Ford management preferred to call the Thunderbird a "personal car." From the time of its introduction until early 1955, the image of the Thunderbird changed from sports car to personal car.

Even before the Thunderbird was being introduced in Ford showrooms, the Chevrolet Corvette was suffering a severe sales drop. The six-cylinder Corvette, with only an automatic Powerglide transmission, and lacking the convenience features of the Thunderbird, went unsold while Thunderbirds enjoyed increasing sales. Corvettes were not selling well, with dealer inventories full, and the storage area at the St. Louis assembly plant full of unsold Corvettes.

With 1955 just around the corner, the future for Corvette did not look bright.

```
#104920-2009


                                           RELEASE ANYTIME
                                           _____


      Ford's new personal car, the all-steel Thunderbird, combines comfort,

convenience and safety with high performance.  It has roll up windows, and

a telescopic steering column.  Hard top or convertible top is optional.




                        - - - - - -




          From the News Bureau
          FORD DIVISION of Ford Motor Company
          P. O. Box 638
          Dearborn, Michigan
```

Aftermarket items

Chapter

25

The Scottop fiberglass top was designed like the stock folding top.

"SCOTTOP" FOR CHEVROLET CORVETTE
1953 thru 1955

Factory photos of the Scottop.

Hardtops

An aftermarket item is an add-on at extra cost device not made by the manufacturer of the vehicle. In automobiles, this covers everything from sun visors, seat covers, mirrors, exterior trim, air conditioning, etc.

In the case of the 1953-54-55 Chevrolet Corvettes, aftermarket items fell into two categories: 1) more power and 2) more convenience. The additional power was supplied to the 1953 and 1954 Corvette six-cylinders by an add-on supercharger. Several companies offered a removable hardtop to increase overall convenience.

In late 1953 or early 1954, McCulloch Motors began fitting 1953 Corvette serial number 24 with a supercharger. The blower unit was placed on the right (passenger) front side of the engine compartment. Ducting carried the pressurized air behind the grille to a manifold which replaced the air cleaners and fed air to all three carburetors. In 1954 a kit was offered, and several 1954 six-cylinder Corvettes became supercharged. The complete

CORVETTE — 1953 thru 1955

FRONT AND SIDE FASTENERS FOR CORVETTE

story of the McCulloch supercharged Corvette six-cylinder engines is found later in this chapter.

Hardtops: There are three basic types built to fit the 1953 to 1955 Corvettes. All are aftermarket items: Corvettes did not have factory built and installed hardtops until 1956.

The first type of hardtop resembles the Corvette folding top in design. There is even a raised crease in the upper rear where the folding top has a bow. This top can be distinguished by a rectangular rear window, similar to the Plexiglas window in the folding top. The main manufacturer was Scottop from southern California. The front of the top fits snugly against the top windshield frame. The inside of this top is painted in a flocked red design. There are three latches, each with a J-bolt and a wingnut. To secure the top, push the sharp point of the J-bolt under the upper windshield frame and tighten it with the wing nut. After a few years, this tends to pull the windshield frame apart.

The Scottop standard model sold for $155 f.o.b. San Diego. The deluxe model was equipped with "two side windows, not portholes" for $225 f.o.b. San Diego.

Colors were primer, pennant blue, Corvette white, Corvette red, gold, bronze, gypsy red, or any standard automobile lacquer. This writer ordered a white Scottop in the summer of 1955. It came in a large box via motor freight. I still have it. I have never seen a deluxe Scottop hardtop with two side windows.

Other manufacturers had tops similar to the Scottop. Acme Fabricating in San Francisco had a top that looked exactly like the Scottop, but we do not know how it fastened in place.

More Scottop details.

The second major type was made by Plasticon in southern California. It has a large wraparound rear window. The front of the top has a lip that fits over the top of the upper windshield frame. There is a large medallion on each side of the top. The Plasticon top uses the stock Corvette folding top latching spots, but has a latching device of its own design. The Plasticon top is much heavier than the Scottop.

The Plasticon hardtop was made in San Gabriel, Calif., and sold for $225. The top's color was Corvette white, unless another color was specified.

The third hardtop is all window, made by Model Builders in Chicago. That is, it is a large bubble, held in place at the stock Corvette folding top latching spots. Not many were made, about 20 we're told.

Back in the '60s the rumor started that the bubble top was actually made for a Bell helicopter. Everyone called it the Bell hardtop. Finally the facts came out: Model Builders built it specifically to fit the Corvette.

An ad for the Plasticon top.

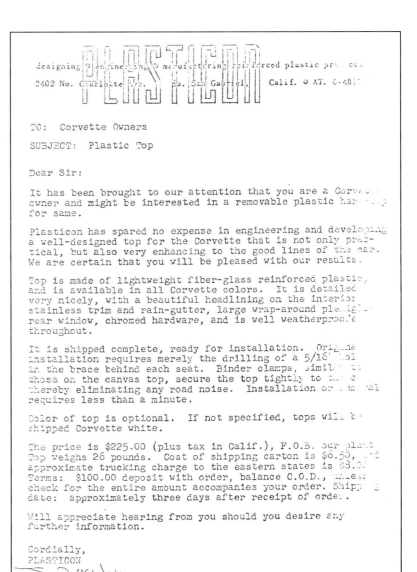

The letter from Plasticon with sales details.

Two Corvettes equipped with Model Builders' tops. The car on the left was painted gun metal gray. It had a tinted top, and was owned by the president of the RC Cola Co. in St. Louis.
The white Corvette is an early '53, owned by Eugene W. Kettering of Hinsdale, Ill. At the time, Kettering was chief engineer of the Electro-Motive Division of GM. This car had a clear Model Builder's top.

Model Builders recalls that it made about 20 tops. About half were clear, while the other half had a green tint. They were expensive, costing about $500.

These tops were great in the winter because the greenhouse effect contributed to the heating of the car. However, since Corvettes of that day were not air conditioned, summer was no time for a clear or tinted plastic top.

One owner of a clear Model Builders hardtop described driving with the top on. He said it was just like riding in a fish bowl!

The clear Model Builders top on Eugene Kettering's 1953 Corvette.

The installation of a tinted Model Builders top.

Other aftermarket ads

Supercharged - McCulloch

The only external sign that a 1953 or 1954 Corvette six cylinder was supercharged was the "Supercharged" nameplate above the front emblem.

April 7, 1954: "The McCulloch Motors Corporation has installed a VS-57 supercharger in a Chevrolet Corvette for the purpose of comparing the relative performance of the car with and without a supercharger.

"The following modifications were prepared in making the experimental supercharger installation.

"Due to the compactness of the engine compartment, location of the blower was necessarily limited to the right side. This necessitated routing the discharge duct forward through the right front air baffle and across to the left baffle where it was brought through at a point opposite, and in line with, the special metal duct constructed to accommodate the three carburetors.

"The supercharger inlet duct was routed through the sheet metal of the right wheel well and connected to a large oil bath air cleaner located at the rear of the wheel well. Protective baffling was installed to shield the air cleaner from road dust."

The above was part of the brochure issued by McCulloch. It also detailed other modifications: spark plugs, distributor, fuel pump, head

The supercharger installation on the McCulloch prototype Corvette, 1953 model serial number 24.

gasket, etc. The idea was to sell McCulloch supercharger kits to the owners of six-cylinder Corvettes. And here was the section that got your attention:

"Performance Data"

"Two significant points are to be found in the following performance curves:

"1. The acceleration time from 9-60 mph was reduced 25% or from 12 to 9 seconds.

"2. The rear wheel horsepower was increased 35% or from 87 to 117."

Well now, these were some real big power improvements. But that was just the results of the supercharged 1953 Corvette. The story of the McCulloch equipped six-cylinder Corvettes began with the start of Corvette production in 1953.

The McCulloch Motors Corporation in California had been developing aftermarket supercharger kits for cars for several years. The installations always resulted in a significant performance improvement. Amid great excitement, they reasoned that the Corvette six cylinder engine's output would show a similar performance improvement. In fact, perhaps Chevrolet would make it an option, to be installed on the Corvette assembly line.

Art Oehrli and his brother, John Oehrli, Jr., had been the brains, as well as the muscle, behind the invention and perfection of the McCulloch supercharger installations. In mid-1953 Art launched a campaign to 1) acquire one of these new Corvette sports cars, 2) fabricate and install a McCulloch supercharger on a 1953 Corvette and provide performance data, and 3) make an arrangement with Chevrolet to install the superchargers on the assembly line as a production line option.

Chevrolet showed some interest in Art's idea for a factory-installed supercharger installation. But first a system had to be installed on a Corvette to prove the expected performance boost. And, as Chevrolet explained gently, there were no cars available.

At the time, in the late summer of 1953, Chevrolet was pooling Corvettes. Production had been slow, and they need a quantity of new Corvettes to introduce to the members of the automotive press on September 28, 1953. Up until the date of the Corvette press party on Sept. 28th, only 38 Corvettes had been built. That's 2-3/4 months of production, at about 14 units per month. Somehow the word slow is inadequate.

Plus, the sales of new Corvettes were carefully controlled to persons of high standing. Mere money was not enough to purchase a new Corvette. Such a controlled sale of a new Corvette was made to the president of the Standard Oil Company of California. The 24th Corvette, serial number E53F001024, was delivered in September of 1953. It may or may not have been at the Sept. 28th press party in Michigan, but that is not clear.

McCulloch Motors was not a high visibility company at the time. It simply could not buy a new Corvette, and there was no such thing as a used Corvette. But John Oehrli, Jr., was a friend of the president of Standard Oil of California (who owned #24). John approached the owner of #24, and after the newness wore off (in a few months), the car was sold to John.

Thus, 1953 Corvette #24 became the test car for the McCulloch prototype supercharger installation. It was involved in all the testing and performance data. As far as we know, only one other 1953 Corvette had a McCulloch supercharger installation. It was serial number 60, E53F001060.

The McCulloch supercharger installation was sold as a kit, shown here on a 1954 Corvette.

Art presented his supercharged Corvette six cylinder performance data to Chevrolet. Although there was some interest shown, Chevrolet did not develop the system as a production option.

Looking back now, we can see their reasons. Corvette sales in April of 1954 were still sluggish. Restrictions on the sale of Corvettes to persons with high visibility positions were being lifted. But Ford had just announced its Thunderbird, which had all those wonderful convenience features. Potential purchasers were taking a "wait and see" attitude.

In the spring of 1954 Zora Arkus-Duntov was employed by the Research & Development Section of Chevrolet Engineering. In 1980 he told this writer that he was working for a while designing school bus drivelines. Mr. Duntov's training as an engineer and experiences as both a race car mechanic and driver gave him a wealth of knowledge. He attended many meetings and represented Chevrolet by presenting discussions on many technical subjects.

In early May Duntov traveled to Los Angeles. He attended a three-day meeting which began on Monday, May 3, 1954. He spoke to two groups, members of the local Society of Automotive Engineers (SAE) and to Cal-Tech students.

Duntov's letter to his boss, Maurice Olley, written May 10, 1954, stated: "I was invited to road test a supercharged Corvette with a McCulloch supercharger. Driving the car, I did not have the impression of increase(d) performance. However, it is my experience that we feel change in acceleration but not the acceleration itself. Therefore, I consider the test irrelevant."

McCulloch had hoped to convince Chevrolet (through Duntov) to install McCulloch superchargers on six-cylinder Corvettes in the factory as an option. So why wasn't Duntov more receptive?

The answer is found in a letter written by Duntov to Maurice Olley on January 22, 1954. After a technical discussion about traction and lateral acceleration, his last sentence was "Furthermore, when Corvette will receive V-8 engine, the power-rear axle load ratio may require attention and having a clearer picture will help." This is admittedly a little confusing because we're taking it out of context. But it does prove that Duntov knew the V-8 was just around the corner back in January of 1954.

Now we can see the picture. McCulloch was developing a power adding option for the six-cylinder Corvette. They asked Duntov to road test it, which he did. But instead of being enthusiastic, he reported it was "irrelevant." The McCulloch folks must have been crushed. But Mr. Duntov was, in effect, telling them not to bother with improving the six cylinder, because a V-8 was on the way. And he found a way to discourage them without telling them anything about the new Chevrolet V-8 engine.

However, McCulloch did develop an aftermarket add-on supercharger kit for the 1954 Corvette. It has been reported that several 1954 Corvettes were modified by the addition of a McCulloch system. The only change in the outward appearance of a McCulloch-equipped Corvette is the addition of the script "Supercharged" on the front of the car, above the front emblem.

By the way, #24 is restored. It lives in southern California and is regularly seen in local shows.

1955 Motorama in New York City

LaSalle II sedan

LaSalle II roadster

The 1953 Motorama had been a huge success. Besides showcasing GM production cars for the public, the dream cars on display generated their own excitement. This public reaction pushed the Corvette into production.

After the 1953 Motorama, Harley Earl's stylists and designers turned to future production cars and dream cars. For the 1954 Motorama, they produced 11 all-new dream cars. A 12th car, the Corvette removable hardtop, was on display but was not called a dream car.

Of the 12 cars on display at the 1954 Motorama, six were Chevrolets or had roots that were traceable to Corvettes or Corvette prototypes.

The 1954 Motorama was another big time success for GM. Harley Earl's design studios began working on dream cars for the 1955 Motorama.

1955 Dream Cars: The Biscayne had a toothy, bulging-eyed front end, designed by Bob Cadaret. The side view showed a four-door hardtop design, with "reverse" side coves. The rear "ducktail" can be traced back to Carl Renner's Corvette Sky-Lite, drawn in 1953. This "ducktail" was used on the 1961 Corvette. The Biscayne was the only Chevrolet dream car built for the 1955 Motorama.

The Biscayne was a one-of-a-kind prototype. It was scrapped in a private salvage yard north of Detroit. Several years ago, the remains of the Biscayne dream car — mostly the front end — were sold by the salvage yard. The Biscayne is being rebuilt by its private owner.

The 1955 Pontiac dream car was the Strato Star, a fiberglass bodied six-passenger coupe. Its side coves can be traced back to Carl Renner's XP-87.

Buick's 1955 dream car was the Wildcat III. Like all the 1955 dream cars, its body was fiberglass. Its styling resembled a slightly customized 1957 Buick convertible. There was one Wildcat III, which was scrapped.

Oldsmobile's contribution was the Delta, a four-passenger coupe. Its fate is unknown.

Cadillac's 1955 dream car was the Eldorado Brougham. It was a predecessor of the production 1957 and 1958 Eldorado Broughams.

The two remaining dream cars revived the name of a previous GM production car — LaSalle. The LaSalle II four-door was a hardtop design. The LaSalle II roadster was a two-seat version of the four-door. Both shared the same front end design. Both had side coves, but the roadster's were very similar to the 1956 Corvette.

Both cars were scrapped, but the remains were saved. Both cars are under restoration in private hands.

The Wildcat III on a show stand.

The 1955 production Nomad was based on the 1954 Corvette Nomad dream car, so the two are close relatives.

The Chevrolet section of the 1955 Motorama.

The Biscayne, a unique dream car.

As the orchestra plays (above) the crowd watches as each GM
Model is displayed on a platform held up by a huge mechanical
arm. The model stands beside a four-door hardtop Buick.

At right: The 1955 Pontiac
display at the Motorama.

The 1955 Pontiac Safari - A sister to the Nomad, thus a relative of the Corvette Nomad.

The 1955 Pontiac Safari sport wagon on display at the Chicago Auto Show.

As the platform revolves, a four-door 1955 Cadillac Sedan DeVille is paraded before an admiring crowd. The LaSalle II coupe is on the platform to the right.

At left. Think the 1955 GM Motorama wasn't big? Look at the crowd waiting to get into the Waldorf Astoria Hotel in New York City. A GM Motorama sign is in the center rear.

Le Mans, France
June, 1955

Chapter

27

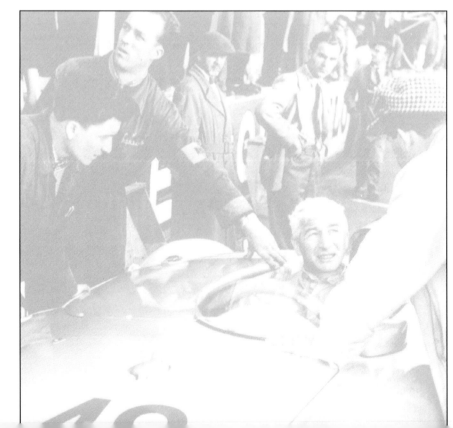

Based on an interview by Jerry McDermott.

June 1955 — Preparations have begun for the 24 hour race at Le Mans, France. Once again Chevrolet's assistant staff engineer, Zora Arkus-Duntov, is on his way to Le Mans to drive for Porsche.

Now we have Duntov's comments from the Jerry McDermott interview:

"Each year the Porsche effort at Le Mans became more intense. For 1955, six Spyders were entered. Three factory Spyders were driven by Pelensky & Von Frankenberg (car no. 37), Glockler & Juhan (car no. 62), and Duntov and Veuillet (car no. 49 - another 1100cc effort). In addition, there were three private teams aided by the factory.

"Any accomplishments in the 1955 race were overshadowed by the tragic crash at 6:28 pm when Pierre Levegh, driving a Mercedes-Benz 300 SLR, hit Lance Macklin's Austin-Healey, which had swerved to avoid Mike Hawthorn. Although Macklin was unhurt, Levegh was killed along with 80 spectators along the fence as his debris plowed into them. At 2 am, on orders from Stuttgart, Mercedes-Benz retired their remaining cars.

"Duntov arrived along the pit straight about two minutes after the accident. He

Duntov discusses race strategy with Dr. Ferry Porsche (in checkered cap).

cleared White House corner and noted a car off the road as well as smoke in the distance. As he made the approach on the straight in front of the pits, he saw that a car had run off the course and into the crowd. His immediate concern was for his wife, so he slowed down. Passing the Porsche pits they waved him on. At the next lap, he again slowed by the pits, looking for his wife, and again the Porsche crew were saying Go-Go-Go. By this time he realized that a Mercedes-Benz was involved in the accident and he speculated that his wife may have been visiting the Mercedes Box as they were friends of their personnel as well. The next lap he continued to search for her, but never saw her until after the race when she came and sat on the car with him and the rest of the team. In the meantime, the Porsche pits were exhorting him as they thought he could win his class.

"This 1955 race was a mixed blessing for Porsche as the accident overshadowed the accomplishment of finishing 4-5-6. Historically, it was Porsche's first victory in the Index of Performance with von Frankenberg and Polenshy driving serial number 550-0046, also placing fourth overall. Their 1500cc entry also beat all the two-liter cars. Duntov repeated as winner of the 1100cc class with serial number 550-0048.

"The Duntov/Veuillet car started 49th of 69 cars and was in 36th place at the end of one hour. At the half way mark they were in 17th place. In the second half of the race, they were as high as 12th place before settling in at 13th and first in class. They averaged 85.48 mph.

"Duntov reported that winning the Index of Performance was worth sizable money to Porsche, which was distributed among all the team drivers. This did not include Veuillet as he wasn't a hired driver.

"After the race Duntov submitted a report, dated July 12, 1955, to his boss at Chevrolet, Maurice Olley, comparing the performance of the 1954 and 1955 Spyders. The letter stated: "Since it will be some time until my report on the European trip will be ready, in the meantime, I would like to tell you about the tail-heavy, directionally stable, and under steering Porsches.

"If you would have driven the cars or could have seen how fast and safe the drivers of average aptitude can drive them now, you would have been very proud. The thorough understanding of mechanics and the effects of roll-coupled distribution that you have given me, paid off in this experiment. The physical changes you know: the stabilizer bar; toe-in and negative camber of the rear wheels — the effect is beyond belief.

"They complain at best what could be described as a lag in response to the steering. The stabilizer could do this by reducing the cornering power of the pair. However, front toe-in geometry, which they have, is at least likely to produce such a lag.

"From my personal observations prior to them mentioning it, I perceived a lag at low steering angles and relatively high lateral G forces in a 120-mph bend. I felt it as a transitional lag and compensated by steering early, but not more than the visual assessment of the bend would demand. They will attempt to isolate the phenomenon and advise the result.

"The next step in the development of Porsche cars will be the increase of static deflection, front and rear, with a simultaneous increase of stabilizer diameter."

Duntov never drove at Le Mans again. During the two years that the Chevrolet engineer drove Porsches, both companies gained. Duntov was indeed a superb driver and engineer.

Racing... Finally

Chevrolet's upper management had no intention of entering racing. For years, their "stovebolt" six earned the reputation of stable, dependable power for Chevrolet's family cars. If one really wanted excitement, there was a Chevrolet convertible coupe. They really didn't give racing a thought.

But Chevrolet's engineers built a lightweight economical V-8 engine. It also happened to be the basis of a very good racing engine.

In 1955, the new V-8 was installed in Chevrolets and Corvettes. No one was more surprised than Chevrolet's upper management when some independent drivers took Chevrolet V-8s stock car racing — and won. They weren't sure that this was good, until the racing successes brought in

A few 1954 and 1955 Corvettes were raced by their private owners with limited successes. Here a C Production Corvette is followed by an Allard at Cumberland Airport on May 15, 1955.

free publicity. When the free publicity showed up as sales at Chevrolet dealers, racing wasn't a bad word anymore.

Sports car racing was another matter. The competition was developed and organized, and Corvettes were not "race ready." But Chevrolet had an engineer with sports car racing experience in Zora Arkus-Duntov. Here's the story of how Duntov got approval to build Corvettes that were competitive.

The trend in the automobile industry in the early fifties was to increase the horsepower slightly every few years. But then Chevrolet Chief Engineer Ed Cole hired Harry Barr. A V-8 engine had been in the works, but it didn't show much promise so it was shelved. Harry Barr's version of a V-8 was light, strong and powerful, the stuff of which legends are made.

With the new V-8 scheduled for production in 1955, there was much

A disguised full-size 1956 Chevrolet's record setting run up Pike's Peak earned attention and publicity for Chevrolet.

Chevrolet's first racing Corvette was this stock-engined 1953, which took some damage.

The Corvette Mule at Phoenix in December of 1955 with Duntov at the wheel. This was the first engine to be equipped with the now famous "Duntov Cam."

Corvette development work to be done. In early 1954 a production Corvette had its six-cylinder engine replaced by a non-operational prototype V-8 engine. This process was called "design check," physically placing a major component in its intended position to look for interferences.

As a functional prototype Chevrolet V-8 engine became available, it was installed in a 1954 Corvette, and assigned the experimental records number EX87. That became its serial number: EX87.

Records are not clear on this point, but EX87 might have been the 1954 Corvette which had been used as a V-8 design check car.

The EX87 Corvette was used in several tests. Because the V-8 was

The **EX87/5951** Corvette mule — with a new body — accelerates during **NASCAR** Speed Week trials. In the background is one of two 1955 Corvettes ordered by Chevrolet engineering; it's shown here with racing stripes and a tail fin. Later, the engine from the mule in the foreground was installed in this car. The fin was removed and the car was assigned number one for the 1956 Sebring Race, where it was driven by Walt Hangsen and John Fitch, and it placed ninth overall.

The Corvette Mule chassis with a new body ran The Flying Mile at Daytona Beach in January of 1956. Here the car starts an acceleration run at the NASCAR Daytona Speed week trials in February. The NASCAR officials' cars in the background are: left to right; 1956 Plymouth Fury, Dodge station wagon.

lighter than the six cylinder, there was a number of suspension tests at the GM Proving Ground in Milford. Apparently no V-8-related suspension changes were made.

The V-8 powered EX87 went through service as a courtesy car in late 1954. Several departments at the GM Tech Center or the GM Proving Ground wanted to try out this new Chevrolet power. In 1955 the car saw occasional use as a V-8 test vehicle.

The new 265-cid Chevrolet V-8 engine was enjoying sudden success in the sales department. A few V-8-powered 1955 Chevrolets were taken to Daytona Beach in February of 1955. This was big time stock car racing, and it got the attention of the public as well as the auto racing world.

During the spring and summer of 1955, Chevrolets competed against Chryslers and Fords. Chevrolets were best suited to short tracks, and they won often.

The performance of the new Chevrolet was big news. This was good news to the folks at Chevrolet Engineering and Chevrolet's ad agency, Campbell-Ewald. They

EX87 serial plate.

EX87 engine compartment — a 1955 air cleaner with 1956 ignition shielding and valve covers, a strange combination.

The EX87 mule car was stripped of its Duntov cam-equipped engine, three-speed transmission and body. The new body, automatic transmission, stock engine and old chassis kept the EX87 serial number and left Chevrolet in 1956. Note 1956 wheel covers.

expanded the news about Chevrolet's racing successes by advertising the NASCAR results in *Motor Trend* and Detroit's trade journal, *Automotive News*. They also had full-page ads in *Road & Track, Popular Mechanics, Life, Boy's Life, Police Chief* and *Law and Order*. Ads in the latter two promoted the Chevy V-8 as a police car.

Chevrolet Engineering and the Campbell-Ewald agency had an idea to get even greater publicity for Chevrolet. They planned to set a new Pike's Peak hill climb record for the upcoming new 1956 Chevrolet.

A 1956 Chevrolet Prototype was available, and with body camouflage added, it could be run before the official release announcement date. Campbell-Ewald contacted Duntov to get his views. He heartily agreed, and, of course, Duntov was to be the driver.

Needing an outside observer, Chevrolet asked NASCAR to witness the runs. On September 9, 1955, Duntov zoomed up the hill in 17 minutes, 24 seconds — a new record! In a publicity blitz, the new record was shouted throughout the country, using ads and articles in magazines and announcements on television.

After the spring, summer and fall races, Chevrolet was established as building a passenger car that could be raced. And, finally, Duntov was recognized as an American race car driver. Up until then, his two wins at LeMans meant little to the average American.

Chevrolet wanted more Corvette race experience, so they used the 1953 Corvette in its inventory, a sports car race was held at the Raleigh Speedway on Saturday, August 20, 1955. Chevrolet's 1953 Corvette came out a bit worse for wear!

Chevrolet was beginning to realize the advertising impact of successful racing. Ed Cole, head engineer, was proud of the extra performance of the 1956 Chevrolet, and the Pike's Peak record-setting run got lots of real attention. Chevrolet and Duntov looked forward to running a Corvette on the sands of Daytona Beach.

The Corvette needed a similar publicity boost, so Duntov again turned to Ed Cole. Duntov had calculated that a Corvette could do 150 miles per hour in a high speed record run. When Duntov suggested a modified Corvette could turn 150 plus miles per hour on the sands of Daytona Beach, Cole was delighted: the project was approved!

To assure the availability of cars for Daytona, two new 1955 Corvettes were ordered in October. They were to be prepared for the races at Daytona.

Also in October, Duntov began modifying EX87, the 1954 Corvette with a V-8 engine. By November, Duntov knew what he wanted — a fiberglass tonneau cover to enclose and streamline the passenger compartment. The stock windshield was to be replaced with a small individual windscreen. A headrest with a large rudder-like fin was added behind the driver's head. The headlights were to be taped over to provide a smooth, drag-free surface. Likewise, the front hood edge and front and rear passenger door edges would be taped over. Parts of the grille would be taped over, with a large enough opening to cool the engine during the standing mile and flying mile runs. The car was fitted with a new 1955 Corvette three-speed manual transmission.

According to Duntov's calculations, he needed about 30 more horsepower than the V-8 was delivering at the time. We must remember that Duntov had tons of experience with pushrod-and-rocker valve heads from his days designing,

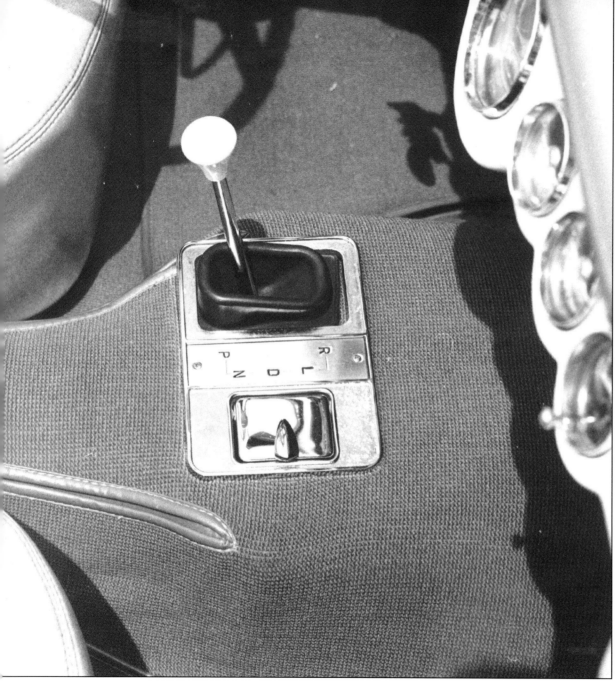

building and maintaining racing engines for Allard and Talbot-Lago and Arden Head Conversions for the Ford flathead.

To get the extra horsepower needed, Duntov designed a new camshaft. It had less lift than the factory high performance cam. Instead, it was designed to match the characteristics of the valve gear. The end result was a valve that opened earlier and closed later, resulting in a fuller valve opening curve.

Duntov's cam was unusual to say the least. In spite of Duntov's growing influence within Chevrolet, he was still a junior staff engineer. That meant everything he did or proposed had to be approved by mid- or upper-level management.

But, finally, the camshaft was approved on a temporary basis. By the time the sample of the cam reached the EX87 "mule" Corvette at the Phoenix proving grounds, it was late November 1955.

Duntov's special cam performed as he had hoped. The engine ran smoothly

EX87 shifter area — like a stock '56 except the gear shift knob is shaped like a '54, but without the shift pattern.

without valve bounce at speeds up to 6500 rpm for long periods of time ...

By early December, Duntov had the EX87 "mule" Corvette running high speed cooling tests at the Mesa Proving Ground. The mule was producing a top speed slightly over 160 mph.

But Duntov calculated that the speed was not enough for the sandy beaches of Daytona. A full belly pan was fabricated for the mule and fastened to the edges of the body.

The belly pan was the answer to increased speed. With the belly pan in place, the EX87/5951 mule produced a top speed of 163 mph. Duntov could do no more.

The EX87/5951 mule was ready for the speed trials in Florida. But the test mule was not to be seen in public. Instead, one of the new 1955 bodies was installed on the modified chassis.

The headrest was installed but later removed. As presented at Daytona Beach, EX87/5951 appeared to be a stock bodied 1955 Corvette with a small, non-stock windshield and a fiberglass tonneau cover over the passenger's compartment; out of sight was the full belly pan.

The headrest must have caused too much drag. After testing it was removed; the mule was ready.

Chevrolet packed up everything and headed for Daytona Beach. By late December 1955 everyone was ready to go, but the weather wasn't cooperating. The sand needed to be hard-packed. A combination of beach sand, wind, tide and tidewater.

The 1956 production Corvette was on the viewing stand at the GM Motorama in New York City when the news came from Florida. Duntov's stock-bodied Corvette just clocked a two-way average speed of 150.583 mph. The folks from Chevrolet were ecstatic.

The next stop for EX87/5951 was the NASCAR Speed Week Trials at Daytona in February of 1956.

The car appeared wearing number 16 with lengthwise racing stripes. There was unusual paint variation — a "side cove" was painted on the side of the 1955 body in a contrasting color, suggestive of a 1956 body side cove. The rest of the February 1956 NASCAR Speed Week concerns 1956 Corvettes, so they will be discussed in the 1956 book.

The EX87/5951 Corvette was used as a mule test car for the 1956 Sebring race. It was used for testing and as a practice vehicle by the Sebring drivers. Meanwhile, four modified production Corvettes were being prepared for the race.

EX87/5951 suffered the indignities expected of experimental, test and race cars. The EX87 chassis, the first to have a Duntov cam, was re-fitted with a new 1955 body. It retained the serial number EX87. Since it left GM in 1956, it has many 1956 features.

The 5951 body was removed and reinstalled on a 1955 Corvette chassis from 1955, serial number 399. This car retained the serial number VE55S001399. The tonneau cover and small windscreen are gone, but the mounting provisions are still there. Likewise, the headrest is gone, but the mounts are there. The full belly pan is still there, a unique item itself.

Both cars — EX87 and '55 S/N 399 — exist in private hands today. When the body from 399 was on the E87 chassis, it was the first vehicle to have the famous cam — now called the Duntov Cam — installed.

Advertisements

Chapter

28

This summer 1954 ad kept the same message as ads had used before! "First of the dream cars to come true." Besides, it stated "so many wanted to drive one that it floored us! — We simply didn't have the cars." and in bold print "Now Being Delivered — you can arrange for a ride today!"

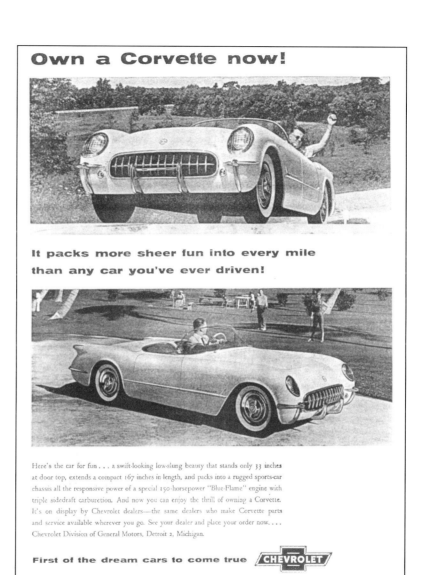

By August, the message was fun: "More sheer fun into every mile ..."

By November, Corvette ads were listing technical details to counter the new Ford Thunderbird, now available at Ford dealers. Strange that the horsepower rating was listed at 150; it had been 155 for several months.

We offer you the most exciting date in town!

Cover one mile in a Chevrolet Corvette . . . and you'll discover that driving has a whole new dimension of delight, a bright new world of pleasure, virtually untapped.

For the Corvette isn't just a new model. It's an entirely new kind of car, a car full of fresh experiences and astonishing abilities.

Those are words — you've heard them used to describe everything from a bucket of bolts to a nine-passenger limousine. But, before you write them off, consider some facts:

The Corvette weighs 2850 pounds. When you tie this to the tail of a 150-horsepower "Blue-Flame" engine you *really* get acceleration . . . a joyous feeling of power that will thrill you.

The Corvette has a 16 to 1 steering ratio. When you flex your wrist on that big vertical steering wheel the Corvette *turns* . . . right NOW . . . with a crisp instant precision you've never experienced.

The Corvette has a 102-inch wheelbase. And there's not an inch of excess overhang. So it moves with the taut alertness of a boxer, keeping its feet wide apart to check body-roll, braced and ready for anything.

The Corvette's center of gravity is only 18 inches above the road. And you can't know what that means until you lance into a curve and sense that unbelievable security, the traction that clings like a cat, the flat "geared-to-the-road" feeling of perfect balance.

These things alone would make a remarkable road car. But the Corvette has much more . . . the liquid smoothness of a special Powerglide automatic transmission . . . individual bucket seats that cradle and brace driver and passenger . . . the terrific impact resistance of a glass-fiber-and-plastic body . . . open-air vision through the deeply curved windshield . . . generous luggage space, luxurious vinyl upholstery and a beautiful bank of instruments that includes a tachometer.

And the Corvette has other pleasures that don't leap to the eye . . . the solid satisfaction of knowing that it is a Chevrolet, with service and parts waiting at virtually every crossroads in America . . . the assurance of durability and long life . . . the reasonable price that stems from Chevrolet's manufacturing skill.

If you want the thrill of driving a real road car you owe yourself an hour with the Chevrolet Corvette. Phone us today . . . and let us set you up with the most exciting date in town.

First of the dream cars to come true

CHEVROLET CORVETTE

SEE YOUR CHEVROLET DEALER

NOVEMBER 1954   21

The one for the road!

 And we mean road . . . for Chevrolet's Corvette is tailored-to-measure for real drivers . . . for those of you whose hearts find a singing lift in the challenge of a winding highway, the call of far blue horizons.

Stay away from this slim temptress unless there's a spark in you that burns bright to the glove fit of a bucket seat . . . to the competent feel of a big 17¼-inch steering wheel . . . to the tingling delight of a car that moves with the cat-quick response of a boxer.

Stay away if your pulse doesn't stir to the silken potency of Corvette's "Blue-Flame" engine, fueling 150 horses through triple carburetors . . . if your heart doesn't soar to the speed-sculptured lines of its sleek plastic body . . . the rake of its fighter-plane windshield.

But if you're a real driver you can't stay away. You'll want to slice through a tight S-turn for the sheer joy of discovering what geared-to-the-road stability means. You'll want to be behind the wheel when the light turns green . . . and the special Powerglide automatic transmission sends you winging, far ahead of the pack. You'll want to tramp on those truck-size brakes for the wonderful feel-ing of security when the Corvette comes smoking down to zero m.p.h. in a dead true line.

But why are we talking when we should be driving? There's a Corvette waiting at your Chevrolet dealer's. The key's in the ignition — and adventure awaits the touch of your toe!

One word before you set out on this date with delight. The Corvette is a *practical* sweetheart. The full measure of Chevrolet's engineering skill was poured into the design of this All-American sports car . . . with all that means in convenience, durability and luxury. Plus this: Swift and experienced service is no farther away than your nearest Chevrolet service department. . . . Chevrolet Division of General Motors, Detroit 2, Michigan.

First of the dream cars to come true

CHEVROLET CORVETTE

December 1954   3

An ad from the December issue of *Motor Trend.* Again the ad brings out the Corvette's fun factor, but lists horsepower at 150 — it should be 155.

Bumpers accent the fenders shape

"Bubble" windshield reduces back-draft

Glass-fiber-plastic body has terrific impact resistance

For experts only!

To put it bluntly, you have to be a better-than-average driver to fully appreciate the pleasures a Corvette can give you. For this is a very special kind of car. It is not a scaled-down convertible . . . it is a sports car, with a crispness of control, a solid "one-piece" way of moving, that go far beyond ordinary experience.

The good driver, stepping into a Corvette for the first time, instantly *knows* the difference. He doesn't ride in this machine . . . he becomes a part of it. It is a direct, vivid extension of his will, an almost-living thing that answers a nudge of the toe, a feather-light pressure on the wheel, with eager precision. The bucket seat molds itself to his back and through it he "reads" the road . . . he knows exactly the position of his car, its balance, the grip on the pavement. No matter how lightning-fast the movement of hand or foot, the Corvette responds . . . right NOW . . . and with hairline

accuracy. And when he punches those big brakes it STOPS, in one solid chunk.

Only the skilled can savor the tremendous margin of safety built in to so responsive an implement. But for them everything about the Corvette is a delight—the tigerish acceleration of the special "Blue-Flame" engine fueled by three side-draft carburetors, the liquid smoothness of the Powerglide transmission, the compactness and terrific impact resistance of the glass-fiber-reinforced plastic body, the utterly individual lines that echo no other car.

If you are such a driver, let us earnestly urge you to make a date with your Chevrolet dealer for a demonstration now. We can promise you a heart-lifting experience that can change your whole concept about the "practicality" of a sports car. . . . Chevrolet Division of General Motors, Detroit 2, Michigan.

CHEVROLET CORVETTE

MOTOR TREND/MARCH 1955   15

This ad from the March 1955 issue of *Motor Trend* refers to the fun one might have driving a Corvette. The same advertisement also stated "it is not a scaled-down convertible ... it is a sports car, with a crispness ..." This is an obvious reference to the Ford Thunderbird.

This ad ran in the April 1955 issue of *Motor Trend*. It mentions a "new 195 horsepower V-8 engine — or the crackling 155 horsepower of the triple-carburetor 'Blue Flame' six." The model illustrated is powered by a six-cylinder engine.

the security of bucket seats

generous luggage space

a tachometer to indicate engine speed

What do you mean, "practical"?

The Corvette is not a "practical" car . . . any more than a sailboat is practical, or a thoroughbred horse, or a pair of skis. It is a sports car, and by its size and nature it is limited to a select group of motorists.

But if you are one of these, and one to whom the art of driving is a source of delight and an exhilarating test of skill . . . then the Corvette becomes a very practical car indeed!

For what is more practical than a car that transforms mere transportation into adventure and puts into the hands of a good pilot the most joyous, responsive, *accurate* road machine he has ever known?

What is extravagant about a car that rewards its owner throughout every minute with rock-solid stability . . . that clings to the pavement like a postage stamp, with razor-sharp 16-to-1 steering ratio and the firecracker reflexes of a polo pony?

What suits the expert driver better than a deep bucket seat, a man-size steering wheel, and, underfoot, the fantastic surge of the Corvette's new 195 horse-power V8 engine—or the crackling 155 horsepower of the triple-carburetor "Blue-Flame" six? What else lifts his heart like the cream-smooth thrust of the special Powerglide transmission, the beartrap grip of the Corvette's husky 11-inch brakes?

For such a driver the Corvette is no extravagance. It is an investment in excitement . . . and one that pays off, every day, in the pure gold coin of pleasure.

If you really enjoy driving, we sincerely urge you to spend an hour at the wheel of a Corvette. There is no other way of discovering the wonderful feeling of exultation a Corvette can give you . . . and keep giving you! Your Chevrolet dealer will be glad to arrange a demonstration. Why not see him soon? . . . Chevrolet Division of General Motors, Detroit 2, Michigan.

CHEVROLET CORVETTE

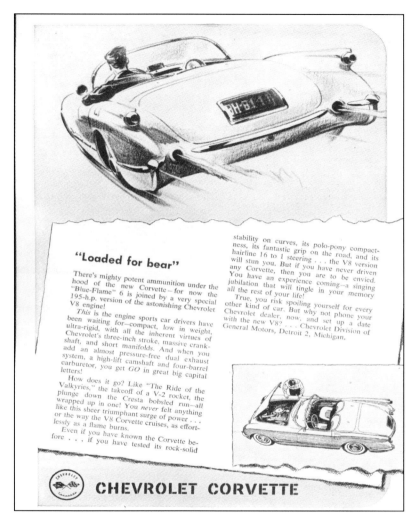

"Loaded for bear"

There's mighty potent ammunition under the hood of the new Corvette—for now the "Blue-Flame" 6 is joined by a very special 195-h.p. version of the astonishing Chevrolet V8 engine!

This is the engine sports car drivers have been waiting for—compact, low in weight, ultra-rigid, with all the inherent virtues of Chevrolet's three-inch stroke, massive crankshaft, and short manifolds. And when you add an almost pressure-free dual exhaust system, a high-lift camshaft and four-barrel carburetor, you get *GO* in great big capital letters!

How does it go? Like "The Ride of the Valkyries", the takeoff of a V-2 rocket, the plunge down the Cresta bobsled run—all wrapped up in one! You *never* felt anything like this sheer triumphant surge of power . . . or the way the V8 Corvette cruises, as effortlessly as a flame burns.

Even if you have known the Corvette before . . . if you have tested its rock-solid stability on curves, its polo-pony compactness, its fantastic grip on the road, and its hairline 16 to 1 steering . . . the V8 version will stun you. But if you have never driven any Corvette, then you are to be envied. You have an experience coming—a singing jubilation that will tingle in your memory all the rest of your life!

True, you risk spoiling yourself for every other kind of car. But why not phone your Chevrolet dealer, now, and set up a date with the new V8? . . . Chevrolet Division of General Motors, Detroit 2, Michigan.

CHEVROLET CORVETTE

This ad ran in the April 25th issue of *Sports Illustrated*. The V-8 engine is mentioned along with the six-cylinder engine. Showing a drawing of a V-8 equipped Corvette, the ad states "... the V-8 version will stun you."

This ad ran in the August 1955 issue of *Motor Trend*. The six-cylinder engine is not mentioned, only "the steel-sheathed fury of 195 V-8 horsepower.

A Corvette is no tame kitten.

Sure, it can purr softly and gently as any household tabby, idling along in the sun. But even so, you catch a hint—a certain lithe competence in the way it moves, an undertone of raw power in the velvety exhaust.

For this one is a tiger! Under its sleek hood beats a savage heart—the steel-sheathed fury of 195 V8 horsepower. Its broad tread clings to the road with an incredible footsureness. And its 16-to-1 steering ratio, the taloned grip of its huge brakes, give it lightning-fast reflexes.

It is a tiger—but an obedient tiger. This fury of acceleration, these whiplash reflexes, are servant to the slightest nudge of your foot, the fractional pressure of your fingers. Your eye and your nerves command these steel muscles with an absoluteness you have never even dreamed.

True, this car can slip through the tangle of traffic with effortless serenity, its special Powerglide transmission metering out a faultless flow of power. In its foam-rubber seats, its deep floor-carpeting, its glove-soft upholstery, are the true marks of luxury.

But the tiger is always there . . . just under the surface. And, if there is fire in your blood . . . if your heart soars to the harsh music of excitement . . . this is the car that was meant for you. Corvette is its name. And *action* is its business. . . . Chevrolet Division of General Motors, Detroit 2, Michigan.

CHEVROLET CORVETTE